SCOTLAND THE BEST
THE ISLANDS

Collins

Published by Collins
An imprint of HarperCollins Publishers
Westerhill Road, Bishopbriggs, Glasgow G64 2QT
www.harpercollins.co.uk
collins.reference@harpercollins.co.uk

HarperCollins Publishers
1st Floor, Watermarque Building, Ringsend Road,
Dublin 4, Ireland

A catalogue record for this book is available from the British Library

ISBN 978-0-00-850528-8

10 9 8 7 6 5 4 3 2 1

Printed in Bosnia and Herzegovina

MIX
Paper from
responsible sources
FSC™ C007454

This book is produced from independently certified
FSC™ paper to ensure responsible forest management.

For more information visit: www.harpercollins.co.uk/green

Caledonian MacBrayne

Caledonian MacBrayne kindly supported
the author's journeys in the Western Isles.

SCOTLAND THE BEST
THE ISLANDS

Peter Irvine

ON ISLANDS

After the lockdowns, I was lucky enough to spend much of the summer of 2021 on islands. We say 'on' never 'in', as in 'living in Edinburgh'. We land on islands, by definition land surrounded by water: the sea in all its caprice, splendour, bounty, peril and drama. It informs all aspects of life on islands, their histories and their potential (the 'green future') and yet every island, even those that are near neighbours, are intrinsically different. We quickly absorb this, for example, on the archipelagos of Orkney and Shetland, the Western Isles and the Small Isles. To live on any small island is to share an indelible connective experience. It's the ultimate in belonging…you belong somewhere. No wonder, with the re-evaluation of life/work in post-Covid times and the growth of island community buyouts and the exciting economic opportunities in the wind and sea on this north-western edge of Europe, Scotland's islands are being viewed though a different lens.

And in this book, through the lenses of inspired photographers, meticulous in their craft and immersed in their subjects, we may see the Scottish islands afresh: their rare beauty, atmosphere and essence. It is a privilege to share these images from such dedicated individuals. Some travel far, camp overnight, all appraise the light, wait for the right moment, give their subjects time and respect and strive for distinction in an Instagram® world.

On Pabay in the Orkney Islands on a warm summer afternoon, we are directed down a track to the shore. There are sheep and birds aplenty, many who've come a very long way; nobody else is around. On a grassy landing above the sparkling sea, we come across the immaculately preserved ruins of one of the oldest homesteads in Europe, older even than the much celebrated Skara Brae on Orkney Mainland. This was a pure island experience I'll never forget.

All the islands offer these kind of moments. They harbour the shared history of time-served communities and their depletion – an often involuntary, perhaps inevitable, depopulation, evidenced by abandoned crofts and shielings. All are home to ubiquitous sheep, myriad birds and distinct fauna and flora that include the machair unique to the northwest. Of many pristine beaches, countless are unvisited. Rocky remote coasts and high cliffs layered in seabirds are often beset by raging seas, sometimes the sea is a mirror that melts into a celestial sunset.

Islands characteristically boast stately lighthouses, triumphs of engineering, as well as historic harbours. The ferry network, past and present, and postboxes in the middle of nowhere, remind us of the abiding importance of connectivity.

Thus the landscapes portrayed in these photographs are etched in the tangible tracks of centuries of human history and, until recently, unchanging nature. Our images point up remote, unheralded places, but we haven't ignored some of the remarkable, but more signposted, 'attractions' where tourists, for good reason, converge.

I hope this portfolio is an encouragement to explore in the footsteps of our photographers with, as we know, an important caveat. While we enjoy and appreciate these islands, we must leave little trace. This book is for everyone who loves Scotland, who loves small islands and revels in the life-enhancing experience of discovering them.

Peter Irvine, Edinburgh, 2022

CONTENTS

LEWIS   11

HARRIS   29

NORTH AND SOUTH UIST AND BARRA   55

SKYE   75

MULL   103

ISLAY   123

ARRAN   145

ORKNEY   161

SHETLAND   189

SMALL ISLES   205

PHOTO CREDITS   240

100 miles

100 kilometres

ATLANTIC OCEAN

NORTH SEA

NORTH CHANNEL

FIRTH OF FORTH

MORAY FIRTH

THE MINCH

SHETLAND ISLANDS
page 189

LERWICK

FAIR ISLE

ORKNEY ISLANDS
page 161

STROMNESS

KIRKWALL

Cape Wrath

Duncansby Head

Butt of Lewis

LEWIS
page 11

HANDA ISLAND
page 230

STORNOWAY

HARRIS
page 29

TARBERT

ULLAPOOL

SHIANT ISLANDS
page 238

ST KILDA
page 10

LOCHMADDY

UIG

NORTH & SOUTH UIST
page 55

PORTREE

INVERNESS

Loch Ness

SKYE
page 75

ABERDEEN

LOCHBOISDALE

BARRA
page 55

CASTLEBAY

THE SMALL ISLES
page 232

MALLAIG

SCOTLAND

COLL

TOBERMORY

TIREE

MULL
page 103

OBAN

EASDALE
page 224

Loch Lomond

COLONSAY

ORONSAY
page 218

BUTE
page 220

GLASGOW

EDINBURGH

PORT ASKAIG

ISLAY & JURA
page 123

GREAT CUMBRAE
page 226

PORT ELLEN

GIGHA
page 228

ARRAN
page 145

OUTER HEBRIDES

INNER HEBRIDES

NORTHERN IRELAND

ENGLAND

ST KILDA

57°48'48"N, 8°35'7"W

The islands of St Kilda are embedded in the heart and soul of Scotland, like no others. Forty miles west of Benbecula, thousands take to the boats every year from Lewis, Harris and the Uists with no certainty that they will even be able to land. However, the islands – Hirta, Boreray, Dun and Soay, and the sea stacks – Levenish, an Armin and Stac Lee, at 165 m the highest in the UK – are spectral and spectacular, thrilling to sail around. They are home to a million seabirds, the most important seabird colony in Northwestern Europe, the clamouring, seething array of gannets around Boreray an unforgettable sight. Diving in the clear waters below is (by all accounts) a similarly quintessential experience. The natural wonders of St Kilda are unique.

Managed by the National Trust, the other aspect of the doubly designated UNESCO World Heritage Site – the human story of St Kilda – is also richly compelling. In Jim Richardson's photograph the historical layout of the village, the streets and the agronomy on the main island, Hirta, are clearly visible (and the juxtaposition of a small cruise ship in the bay). Inhabited for two millennia, its population peaking in the late 17th century, Hirta was abandoned by a vote of the parliament of the 36 folk still living here in 1930, a significant milestone in the depopulation of Northwest Scotland – always a nationally sensitive issue. Now what remains is a somewhat incongruous military presence (since 1957) and archaeologists and scientists are the part-time residents. But St Kilda will always inspire and intrigue.

PHOTOGRAPH **JIM RICHARDSON**

LEWIS

58°8'02"N,
6°39'16"W

LEWIS

The ferry to Lewis from Stornoway is the biggest in the Calmac fleet; you arrive at Stornoway's bustling waterfront in the largest town in the Hebrides. Lews Castle, once the home of Sir James Matheson, the opium mogul, sits above the town in its extensive grounds: a parkland for walking and golf. From Stornoway, roads go west to Great Bernera and the idyllic beaches around Uig, via the spot where the renowned carved Lewis Chessmen were unearthed, and northwest to the Callanish Stones and the 'Blackhouse Village', now a boutique stayover. Finally, further north is the Butt of Lewis, often thrashed by stormy seas. A few miles northeast from Stornoway are the less celebrated but fine beaches of Tolsta, Traigh Mhòr and Ghearadha. South is the road to Harris and its mountains.

Lewis was once part of the Kingdom of the Isles and the Norse influence is everywhere, as is Gaelic culture and language and also the Presbyterian tradition. Visitors may find it quaint or sometimes inconvenient to find that the Sabbath is still observed.

Quite separate from anything on the mainland, both a rich contemporary and a traditional culture is well in evidence. In Stornoway, An Lanntair is the principal arts hub of the Hebrides, with exhibitions, performance art, a bookshop and a restaurant. Every year a big open-air (tented) festival, HebCelt, is held in the Castle grounds. And on Lewis, Peter May's books are ubiquitous, as are the crime scenes he describes.

There is a lot of bog on Lewis, a lot of glorious beach around the edges and a lot of Lewisian gneiss, rock as old as it gets. It's not the easiest terrain in which to find a purchase but ancient history, myth and legend define Lewis and pride and respect for the land run deep.

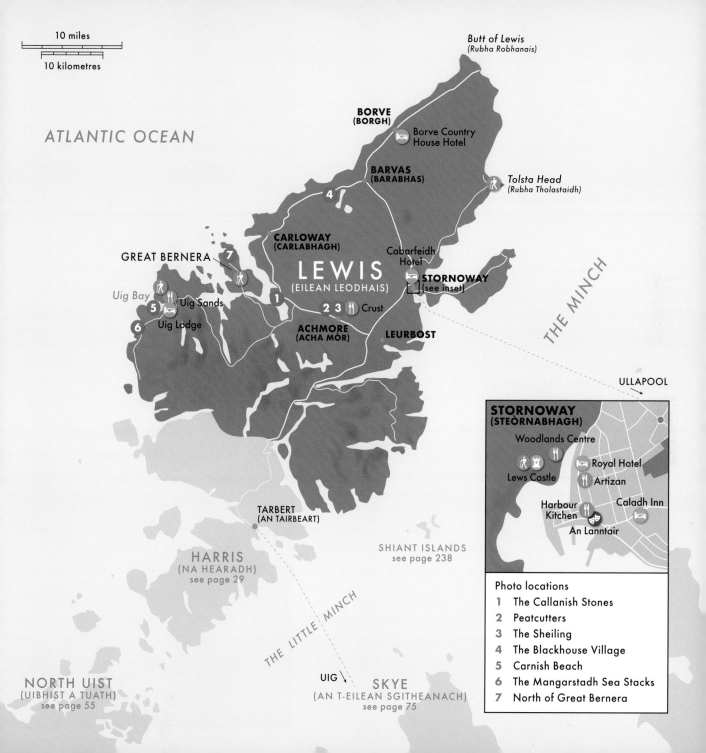

10 miles

10 kilometres

ATLANTIC OCEAN

Butt of Lewis
(Rubha Robhanais)

BORVE
(BORGH)

Borve Country
House Hotel

BARVAS
(BARABHAS)

Tolsta Head
(Rubha Tholastaidh)

4

CARLOWAY
(CARLABHAGH)

LEWIS
(EILEAN LEODHAIS)

Cabarfeidh
Hotel

STORNOWAY
(see inset)

GREAT BERNERA

7

THE MINCH

Uig Bay

5   Uig Sands

1

2 3   Crust

6   Uig Lodge

ACHMORE
(ACHA MÒR)

LEURBOST

ULLAPOOL

TARBERT
(AN TAIRBEART)

SHIANT ISLANDS
see page 238

STORNOWAY
(STEÒRNABHAGH)

Woodlands Centre

Royal Hotel

Lews Castle

Artizan

Harbour
Kitchen

Caladh Inn

An Lanntair

HARRIS
(NA HEARADH)
see page 29

THE LITTLE MINCH

UIG

SKYE
(AN T-EILEAN SGITHEANACH)
see page 75

NORTH UIST
(UIBHIST A TUATH)
see page 55

Photo locations
1   The Callanish Stones
2   Peatcutters
3   The Sheiling
4   The Blackhouse Village
5   Carnish Beach
6   The Mangarstadh Sea Stacks
7   North of Great Bernera

THE CALLANISH STONES

58°11′51″N, 6°44′43″W

The Callanish Stones are the most well-known and visited attraction of the Hebrides. The site, about 12 miles from Stornoway, is well signposted. Older than Stonehenge, there are 13 standing stones in a cruciform formation around a central monolith and many other ritual stone sites nearby, including Callanish II and Callanish III a kilometre away, thought to be the most impressive. God knows how or why they got here over 5000 years ago but archaeologists in the mid-1980s suggested that 'every 18.6 years when the full moon was low in the sky, the light danced along the edges of the stones'. Or they mark the sites of massive lightning strikes. There's a wee café and a shop.

Richard Cross on one of his cycling expeditions to the Hebrides was looking for a quiet place to set up his tent. Once the last tour busses had gone, he made a discreet pitch and found himself alone in this ancient landscape. God was on his side, the sunset lasted well into the night.

PHOTOGRAPH **RICHARD CROSS**

PEATCUTTERS

58°10'18"N, 6°34'36"W

Peat has been the fuel of the Western Isles since the forests were cleared. For generations, the annual tradition of peat cutting has been an integral part of life. Starting on a weekend in May, the peat is sliced and thrown aside, laid out on the moor to dry, turned, and then gathered in at the end of summer to be stacked out the back of your house and that of your neighbours. It's a community project in every sense: collective human energy bringing it home, releasing organic energy as it burns in the stove.

Mhairi Law is not in the photograph, but these are her friends, caught in an activity that has its own joie de vivre. The allocated peat hang of her family is here at Acha Mòr, where Mhairi now has a studio – the Island Dark Room – for her photography and other crafts work, including hand-made designs with tweed.

PHOTOGRAPH **MHAIRI LAW**

THE SHEILING

58°11′15″N, 6°31′48″W

The sheiling is not a croft but a summer house for cattle and sheep. As with the vignette of peat cutting on the previous page, this photograph of an isolated house over the hill near Acha Mòr reminds us that the Old Ways are still part of the landscape of Lewis visible around the A858, which cuts through the island's heartland. They can seem to merge into the stony land.

Sheilings are rough and ready, for animals rather than their keepers, though butter and curd cheese might have been made and shelter taken. There are few windows and a tin roof often needing repair. Most have not yet been turned into homes or made fashionable as in 'bothy culture'. It has been suggested that they were useful for dalliances or 'sexual experimentation', as writer Derek Cooper put it, though what that implies is not clear. In any case they provide a respite from the midges.

PHOTOGRAPH **MHAIRI LAW**

THE BLACKHOUSE VILLAGE

58°17'47"N, 6°47'27"W

The Gearrannan Blackhouse Village in the northwest of Lewis is just that: a village of squat, thatched cottages, dark inside and out. But it would be hard to find a more atmospheric retreat in the Hebrides (or on any island). Mainly available for holiday accommodation, the rooms are basic but real-fire warm and cosy. It is almost as if you are living in thon times; you wake to the crashing Atlantic foam. Near the Callanish Stones and the earth-floored, just-as-it-was Blackhouse of Arnol (a museum), the village is far from the sodium lights of Stornoway and the rest of the damned world.

PHOTOGRAPH **PAUL TOMKINS**

CARNISH BEACH

58°10'52"N, 7°3'18"W

Carnish (or Carnais) Beach is one of the many alluring beaches that stretch from Timsgearraidh to Mangarstadh around Uig Bay, less than an hour from Stornoway. It's well known for snorkelling and swimming.

Photographer and artist Matthew Dalziel and partner Louise Scullion, who have a house nearby, are well familiar with the aspects, the weather and the natural world of this coast. Sea eagles fly over. This photograph captures an intriguing pattern of seaweed in the clear water.

PHOTOGRAPH **DALZIEL**

THE MANGARSTADH SEA STACKS

58°9′03″N, 7°6′24″W

The coast around Uig is not all glorious beaches. The drama of the Mangarstadh (or Mangersta) Sea Stacks could not be further away from the gentle sandy strand of the same name, though they are only 2 km further on along the B8011. Both stacks and beach begin at small pull-in car parks, where short paths begin.

Michael Stirling-Aird found this vantage point almost by accident while on holiday. There's a lay-by and the path to the sea, but no indication of the cliffs until their grassy tops come into view after a few hundred yards. You might marvel at the grandeur of these timeless pinnacles, that they are so unknown, or just at the indomitable endurance of Lewisian gneiss.

On the way here, also tucked away but increasingly well known (you should book well ahead), is the superlative seafood restaurant with the view to die for – Uig Sands.

PHOTOGRAPH **MICHAEL STIRLING-AIRD**

NORTH OF GREAT BERNERA

58°13'48"N, 6°50'37"W

Great Bernera or just Bernera (though it is, of course, great), reached by a road bridge built in 1953, is on the sea loch Ròg (Roag). Around 250 people live here on an island steeped, as they say, in history. In 1874, in what became known as 'The Bernera Riot', the crofters resisted the heavy-handed Clearances of their livestock from their land to make way for a sporting estate, exposing the corruption of the land-owning class, in particular the nasty Sir James Matheson (who also owned Lewis, having made his fortune in opium) and won a court case that paved the way for Scottish land reform.

In the north of the island the very fine Bostadh (Bosta) beach is known by some as 'Paradise'. Richard Cross camped nearby (obviously on a very fine day) and took this photograph of the offshore islets. Somewhere in this turquoise-blue seascape is Marcus Vergette's Time and Tide Bell. Built on a skerry, chiming at high tide, it is the second of twelve in an ongoing installation project (since 2010) around the UK coast.

PHOTOGRAPH **RICHARD CROSS**

LEWIS: THE BEST OF

WHERE TO STAY

ROYAL HOTEL, STORNOWAY www.royalstornoway.co.uk. 01851 702109. The most central and urbane of the 3 main hotels in town all owned by the same family. Boatshed Bistro and HS-1 offer ok choice for dining. • The **CABARFEIDH HOTEL** www.cabarfeidh-hotel.co.uk. 01851 702604, prob the best rooms. • The **CALADH INN** www.caladhinn.co.uk. 01851 702740. This hotel (pron 'Cala') and its café are prob best value. These are among the few places open on Lewis on a Sunday. The Royal has the best buzz. • **BORVE COUNTRY HOUSE HOTEL, BORVE, NORTH LEWIS** www.borvehousehotel.co.uk. 01851 850223. 20 miles N of Stornoway. Contemporary, perhaps a bit soulless with boutique-style rooms. Bar and restaurant busy with locals at weekends. • **UIG LODGE, UIG** www.uiglodge.co.uk. On a headland way out west with some view! Accom in lovely rooms available when not booked for exclusive use like fishing parties. A remarkable landmark lodge, comfortable and with intimate dining. • **LEWS CASTLE** www.lews-castle.co.uk. 01625 416430. Grand 'castle' mansion with historic public rooms, café and upstairs, an apartment hotel with some rooms by the night. Top views of the waterfront and town. Good breakfast in the WOODLANDS CENTRE (200 m).

WHERE TO EAT

HARBOUR KITCHEN, STORNOWAY 01851 706586. Nr harbour. Excellent seafood bistro. • **UIG SANDS, UIG** www.uigsands.co.uk. 01851 672334. Far west but worth the drive for one of the best seafood restaurants in Scotland and an incredible view. Contemporary building and menu. • **ARTIZAN, STORNOWAY** 01851 706538. Church St café/restaurant/wine bar. Conscientious home cooking, good buzz, best coffee. Cl Sun. • **CRUST, ACHA MÒR** on the A858 west, 20 mins from Stornoway. Roadside takeaway crusty trusty pizzas, all the right ingredients. 12–7.30 pm. Cl Sun.

WHERE TO WALK

BEACHES OUT WEST: Around Uig via B8011 (a good road), CARNAIS, ARDROIL and MANGARSTADH, one of the furthest west beaches in the UK (and Europe). • **TOLSTA HEAD** (a wild headland) 10 miles NE of Stornoway and the stacks of Heisgeir, then to stunning TRAIGH MHOR beach extending to GHEARADHA turning back to NORTH TOLSTA and Lord Leverhulme's folly, the Bridge to Nowhere. Consult locally or maps for directions. 3 hours. • **LEWS CASTLE GROUNDS**. Many pathways, good waymarking but can do a 2-hour circular walk with great views. WOODLANDS CENTRE for sustenance. • **GREAT BERNERA TRAIL** (circular) starting from GB Community Centre (café), consult for directions, don't miss pristine beach at BOSTADH. Circular 4 hours.

HARRIS

57°49'49"N,
6°54'49"W

HARRIS

Harris, an island of two halves: two entities, North and South, one mountainous, one more low-lying, but with two distinctly different coastlines – the extraterrestrial east, and the west with some of the best beaches in the world. From north to south you travel from rugged to refined, from land massif to the water world of the Uists, from decidedly Protestant to increasingly Catholic. All this contrast makes for a fascinating divergence of experience and scenery. Next to Skye, Harris is probably the most photographed of Scottish islands.

Tarbert in the middle, where the ferry leaves for Uig in Skye is the largest settlement, with two good hotels, a short hop to Scalpay, the Harris tweed shops and the new distillery about to distribute its long-matured, already highly praised whisky. Leverburgh, where the ferry leaves for Berneray and the Uists is 23 miles south via the famous beaches, a great (and one of the original) country house hotels, a uniquely charming golf course and a brilliant takeaway café at Northton. On the other coast, the Golden Road south is one of Scotland's most scenic routes, at times astonishing. Both coast roads take you to Rodel. Few places make you feel so much at the end of the road: a lonely harbour, an empty hotel, an extraordinary church and an atmosphere of the land time forgot.

5 miles

5 kilometres

LEWIS
(EILEAN LEODHAIS)
see page 11

SCARP
(AN SGARP)

HUSHINISH
(HUISINIS)

GLEN ULLADALE

North Harris
Eagle Observatory

ATLANTIC
OCEAN

TARANSAY
(TARASAIGH)

7

Harris
Hotel

6

Hotel Hebrides

LUSKENTYRE
(LOSGAINTIR)

Harris
Distillery

TARBERT
(AN TAIRBEART)

North Harbour Bistro

11

9

SCALPAY
(EILEAN SCALPAIGH)

HARRIS
(NA HEARADH)

8

Scarista Beach

10

Scarista House

Temple/Croft 36

NORTHTON

Golden Road

LEVERBURGH
(AN T-OB)

UIG, SKYE

2

The Butty Bus/
The Anchorage

RODEL
(ROGHADAL)

4

BERNERAY
(BHEARNARAIGH)

SOUND OF HARRIS

3   5

Renish Point
(Rubha Reinis)

1

NORTH UIST
(UIBHIST A TUATH)
see page 55

THE LITTLE MINCH

Photo locations

1   The Ferryman
2   The Butty Bus
3   Rodel Churchyard
4   House in South Harris
5   Rodel Harbour
6   Luskentyre
7   River and Sand
8   Harris Golf Course
9   Scalpay
10 Scarista Post Office
11 VW Campers

THE FERRYMAN

57°42'10"N, 7°10'49"W

Donald is the ferryman on the Calmac boat to Berneray and has plied the Sound of Harris since 1996, just possibly crossing this stretch of the Atlantic more than anybody else. Previously it was only a passenger boat service, now it's one of the full car- and truck-carrying lifelines in the Hebrides.

Calmac sponsored my travels round the Scottish Islands in the summer of 2021, but I have no reservations about highlighting the ferries here and elsewhere in the book. Though beset with unforeseen challenges more than ever in this year, and clearly delays and cancellations happen, I'd declare that in years of ferrying me to the islands, they have not let me down once (or hit the quay). So I'm unequivocal in my appreciation for the crews on these short island-to-island journeys. While they get on with the routine of sailing and servicing a ship, you take the fresh air and the sun and the views on deck looking out for dolphins and porpoises, or chill out below with a book or a beer and a Calmaccy Cheese.

I know this is a romantic view in itself, but to my mind there's simply no better way to arrive, anywhere.

PHOTOGRAPH **JOHN MAHER**

THE BUTTY BUS

57°46'02"N, 7°1'29"W

The Butty Bus, parked at the Leverburgh Pier for ten years, is the well-loved food stop as you wait for the ferry to Berneray and the Uists, unquestionably a local attraction and a place to hang out. Photographer John Maher has a workshop by the quayside and is often in the queue for soup and a butty.

Chris Ross acquired the bus that originally came from the Rolls-Royce plant in Crewe and was then used for film-set catering, so it was fitted out with a kitchen before it got to this end of the world.

Though a long-standing feature, the Butty Bus has moved with the times. You can order and sit in your car and Chris will message you when your fish 'n' chips is ready.

PHOTOGRAPH **JOHN MAHER**

RODEL CHURCHYARD

57°44'28"N, 6°57'47"W

St Clement's Church by Rodel in the far south of Harris is a classic island kirk in a Hebridean landscape. It's worth making the circuit via either the Golden Road or the A859 by the beaches, just to visit this well-preserved ancient edifice of Lewisian gneiss built for the Macleod Clan Chiefs of Harris. Many of them are in the graveyard.

Probably influenced by Iona Abbey and dating from the early 16th century, it has an elegant cruciform structure and a tower that the adventurous might climb. Empty and atmospheric, it contains blackened effigies and important ornamental sculpture. It's spooky but also edifying.

Goats in the graveyard graze among the headstones of the young Harris lads lost at sea in the Great War. There are other fallen angels on the outside of the tower.

PHOTOGRAPH **PAUL TOMKINS**

HOUSE IN SOUTH HARRIS

57°44'37"N, 6°57'56"W

Julian Calverley is a master of creating a mood, conveying an atmosphere, especially in a rural landscape. 'Delicately balancing his control over light, palette and composition', he has been exhibited and published and won many awards. Harris is rich in subject matter for Julian, in stark scenery and juxtaposed human intervention.

This isolated house under a brooding sky is darkly poignant. It just wouldn't be as powerful an image on a good day.

PHOTOGRAPH **JULIAN CALVERLEY**

RODEL HARBOUR

57°44'16"N, 6°57'41"W

Another image by photographer Julian Calverley that conveys something quite different from the sunny blue-sky, blue-sea pictures usually associated with the west coast and its gently lapping sea. But nevertheless this too is forthrightly Harris, the harbour at the end of the road: the Golden Road that is, one of the most dramatically scenic coasts in Scotland.

Rodel itself often has an abandoned air about it. The church is elegiacally beautiful, the nearby saltpans strange, the once notable hotel refurbished for private use. This boat looks as if it might be about to set off across the Styx, the boundary between the Earth and the underworld. Or maybe it's about to go fishing.

PHOTOGRAPH **JULIAN CALVERLEY**

LUSKENTYRE

57°53'03"N, 6°56'42"W

The legendary beach at Luskentyre: the one on your bucket list that you must visit one day, the one that lends itself to so many brilliant photographs, the beach in your January dreams.

It's one of the first beaches you come upon on the A859, over the hill from Tarbert on the road south that also goes by Seilebost, Horgabost, Borve and Scarista. All beautiful.

Richard Cross's drone shot shows the beach at its most resplendent, mesmerizing, almost abstract, the sea unnaturally blue (and there are no filters). Save for the hazy purple mountains, this could be the Caribbean.

PHOTOGRAPH **RICHARD CROSS**

RIVER AND SAND

57°54'0"N, 6°54'51"W

Taken from a hill, Beinn Dhubh on the road south from Tarbert, this photograph of the coast most associated with wide sandy beaches shows a different aspect of west South Harris.

The palette of colours and the liquid light looking southwest towards Toe Head, where the river spills into the sea at Sheileboist, create an image that seems almost to be a painting. The softly textured landscape is a long way from the mighty mountains of North Harris and from the middle moorlands of Lewis, where Mhairi Law hails from.

PHOTOGRAPH **MHAIRI LAW**

HARRIS GOLF COURSE

57°49'55"N, 7°2'12"W

The steep course at Scarista is one of the most remote, most enchanting and most spectacular of golf courses. On the main A859, its nine unpredictable holes, none without challenges, slope down to the sea and overlook the famously fabulous Scarista Beach. The first tee has one of the great views in golf.

To play, you just turn up, get out of the car and put 20-odd quid in the box, no need to book. It's basic but testy. As is shown, it's not 'open' on Sundays. It would beyond churlish to break that rule.

Richard took this picture passing by on his 40th birthday bike trip. He didn't have his clubs with him.

PHOTOGRAPH **RICHARD CROSS**

SCALPAY

57°51'55"N, 6°40'15"W

Scalpay, an island, is a short skelp (5 miles) from Tarbert. You cross a bridge (built in 1998) to find a thriving community of fisherfolk, artists and craftspeople in a neat little world of its own. There's an impressive lighthouse, one of the original Northern Lighthouses dating back to 1788, with a tower by Robert Stevenson added in 1824. There's a circular walk to it through moorland and machair, boat trips go around it in summer.

Scalpay is also the home of a highly-thought-of café/restaurant – The North Harbour Bistro and Tearoom. It's best to book. All in all, Scalpay is a pretty cool place to spend a day. Hang out longer and you might just want to live there.

PHOTOGRAPH **PAUL TOMKINS**

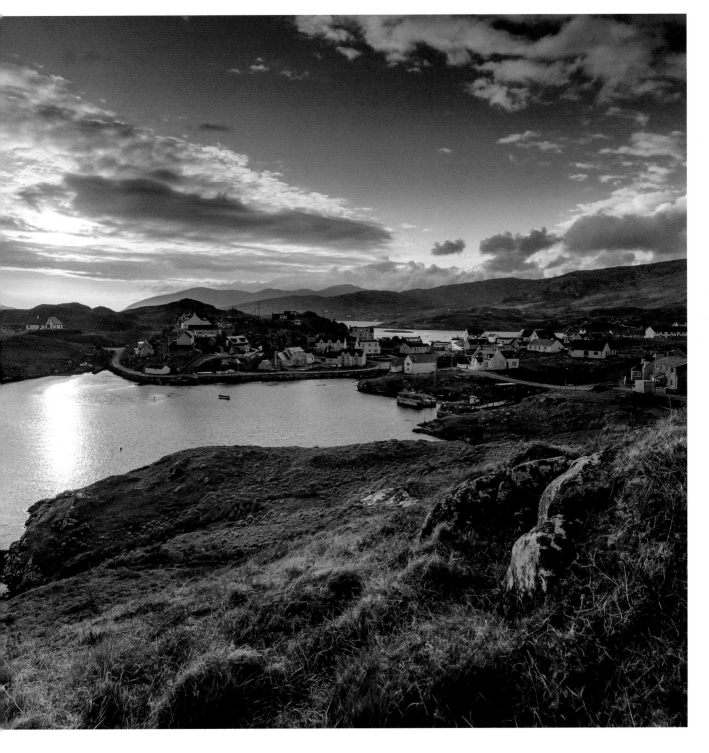

SCARISTA POST OFFICE

57°50'11"N, 7°0'44"W

John's picture shows South Harris in winter. Life goes on. He lit the
sign specially, though the light in the phone box goes on by itself.
It's still there, though the post office has become a craft/tweed shop.

Near Scarista House, one of Scotland's first notable rural hotels, and
across the road from the beach, you'd hardly notice the post office
if you didn't live here. There is no actual township. Perhaps that's
why it's closed. Shame really, but a long way from long summer
days and tourists wandering through, life does go on.

PHOTOGRAPH **JOHN MAHER**

VW CAMPERS

57°51'42"N, 6°58'39"W

Here on Harris's golden coast there's now a busy happy campsite at Horgabost (not in picture), where campervans aplenty pitch up for a couple of nights. I confess I'm not a huge fan of the campervan revolution, whereby some folk hire a monstrous motorhome down south and drive north hoping to enhance their room...with a view. Getting stuck behind one, or several campervans, especially drivers who refuse to stop and let people past, can be stressful for the rest of us, especially if you live down that single-track road.

But this picture by John Maher, taken a couple of years before the convoy set off, remind us of the attraction of independent travel and how idyllic and exhilarating it can be. Beautiful VWs, a great location: the aesthetic is scintillating. It could have been an ad, one that I would have bought into.

I do know there are many conscientious considerate travellers with personalized unobtrusive vehicles they love. You are welcome to share the Highlands and the Islands, guys. Just pull over sometimes.

PHOTOGRAPH **JOHN MAHER**

HARRIS: THE BEST OF

WHERE TO STAY

SCARISTA HOUSE, nr **SCARISTA BEACH** www.scaristahouse.com 01859 550238. Comfy, laid-back, tasteful family home. Individual everything. Great dinner. 12 miles S of Tarbert. • **HOTEL HEBRIDES, TARBERT** www.hotel-hebrides.com 01859 502364. Contemporary, very well run, boutique-style hotel at the quayside where the big ferry to Skye leaves from its new terminal. Good rooms and restaurant, locals' bar. Heart of the matter in Tarbert. • **HARRIS HOTEL, TARBERT** www.harrishotel.com. 01859 502154. A contrast to Hebrides above but another well-run family hotel with great comfy public rooms and a wonderful garden. Trad values. Range of rooms.

WHERE TO EAT

All recommended hotels-especially Scarista • **NORTH HARBOUR BISTRO, SCALPAY** 01859 540218. 20 mins from Tarbert. Overlooks the Harbour. Local and islandwide rep for sourced, chef-led, proper food. Top spot. Cl Mon • **TEMPLE, NORTHTON** 07487 557626. 3 miles N of Leverburgh, 1 ml off main rd. Brilliant café/ takeaway with superb home baking: bagels/cinnamon buns/brioches/pastries (all the cool stuff) and soups. Great view from outside tables. Daytime only, open Sun. • **THE ANCHORAGE, LEVERBURGH** 01859 520225. At the quayside where the ferry leaves, a quite brilliant terminal café. Home-made food and bar. • **CROFT 36, NORTHTON** www.croft36.com. 01859 520779. Mile off the main A859. A shack (not staffed), where they leave excellent homemade food: bread, pies, cakes, ready made. Daytime only.

WHERE TO WALK

The **NORTH HARRIS EAGLE OBSERVATORY, HUISINIS** and **GLEN ULLADALE, NORTH HARRIS**: three great separate walking spots all down the single-track B887 N of Tarbert on the A859. • The Observatory starting place is first, 3 miles along. There's a parking place with an interpretation board at a bend in the road at the foot of Glen Miabhaig. 3 mls, 2 hrs. • Huisinis is at the end of the road, 13 miles, beaches at the start and the walk to Crabhadail. 5 mls return, 3 hrs. Glen Ulladale starts just before Abhainn Suidhe big house (you pass the door), up the road to the power station and dam. Beyond is the glen with the biggest rock overhang in Europe, stags and eagles. • Trailboards for walks at all the southern beaches. • From Rodel, the walk to Renish Point, the furthest southerly point starting at St Clement's Church, is a wild coastal treat.

NORTH AND SOUTH UIST AND BARRA

57°27′04″N,
7°18′06″W

NORTH AND SOUTH UIST AND BARRA

In an archipelago stretching 130 miles, the Uists North and South, from Berneray through Benbecula to Barra and on to Mingulay, are the very epitome of the Outer Hebrides: the Western Isles. An abiding impression of the journey to and across them, on small ferries and causeways (constructed over only the last 60 years), is that the sea is omnipresent. There are also over 800 freshwater lochans.

This is the very Atlantic edge where live the farthest-flung and scattered communities in Western Europe. You cross the Sound of Harris or the Sound of Barra to a distinctly quieter place, fringed with exquisite beaches, where you can hear every movement of the sea and the gulls, perhaps even the elusive corncrake, one of Britain's rarest birds. Berneray, close to the ferry port from Harris and linked by a causeway, has a special atmosphere and completeness all of its own and a long west-facing beach with sunsets to soothe the soul.

Far south, Barra is encompassed by a circular road, so you can cycle around it in a couple of hours. Heaval (383 m) overlooking Castlebay, provides a panorama from Kisimul Castle in the bay to Barra's famous 'airstrip on a beach' to the north and to Vatersay, the Western Isles', most southerly inhabited island. There you cross by a causeway to an isthmus bounded by unique east- and west-facing crescent beaches.

Further south still the tiny, faraway island of Mingulay, whose last residents left over 100 years ago (in 1912) can be reached by boat trips from Barra or South Uist.

As you make the journey across the Uists there is a powerful sense of being on the margin, of making an almost spiritual, as well as a corporeal, connection between yourself, the land and the sea.

10 miles

10 kilometres

PABBAY
(PAB AIGH)

LEVERBURGH
(AN T-ÒB)

HARRIS
(NA HEARADH)
see page 29

SOUND OF HARRIS

BERNERAY
(BHEARNARAIGH)

BORERAY
(BORARAIGH)

3

THE LITTLE MINCH

Balranald
Nature Reserve

Hamersay House
Barpa Langass

LOCHMADDY
(LOCH NAM MADADH)

Langass Lodge

UIG (UIGE)

MONACH ISLANDS
(NA H-EILEANAN MONACH)

BALESHARE
(BAILE SEAR)

NORTH UIST
(UIBHIST A TUATH)

The Stepping Stone

Culla Bay

2

6

GRIMSAY
(GRIOMASAIGH)

SKYE
(AN T-EILEAN SGITHEANACH)
see page 75

ATLANTIC OCEAN

BENBECULA
(BEINN NA FAOGHLA)

CLACHAN

HOWMORE
(TOBHA MOR)

SOUTH UIST
(UIBHIST A DEAS)

SEA OF
THE HEBRIDES

7

LOCHBOISDALE
(LOCH BAGHASDAIL)

POL A' CHARA

Polochar Inn

SOUND OF BARRA

ERISKAY
(EIRIOSGAIGH)

THE SMALL ISLES
(NA H-EILEANAN TARSAINN)
see page 232

OBAN

BARRA
(BARRAIGH)

Isle of Barra
Beach Hotel

Heaval

1

CASTLEBAY
(see inset)

8

OBAN

VATERSAY
(BHATARSAIGH)

SANDRAY
(SANNDRAIGH)

CASTLEBAY
(BÀGH A' CHAISTEIL)

4 Café
Kisimul

PABBAY
(PABAIGH)

MINGULAY
(MIUGHALAIGH)

5

BERNERAY
(BEÀRNARAIGH)

Kisimul Castle

OBAN

Photo locations
1 Barra Airport
2 Benbecula Sunset
3 The Coralbox, Berneray
4 Castlebay and Kisimul, Evening
5 Mingulay
6 The Road
7 The Machair
8 Vatersay

BARRA AIRPORT

57°1′32″N, 7°26′58″W

Barra Airport is probably one of the most quietly famous airports in Britain; certainly it's among the most charming. Situated on the wide shallow bay of Traigh Mhor at the northern tip of the island, it's not much more than an airstrip on the beach and flights are dependent on the tide as well as the wind. Some folk (about 10,000 a year) come to Barra just to arrive this way. It is a Loganair scheduled flight from Glasgow.

It's also known as Cockle Beach Strand and foragers can often be seen gathering the sweet little shellfish in the winter months. Some end up on the menus at the Castlebay and Isle of Barra Hotels.

By air to and from Barra is an adventure, just remember you may be staying longer than you intended. Maybe not such a bad thing!

PHOTOGRAPH **STEFAN AUTH**

BENBECULA SUNSET

57°27′31″N, 7°24′06″W

Benbecula in the watery heartland of North Uist is a community defined by its long association with its military airport and the Ministry of Defence. It's also a community hub for all of the Uists: the Co-op, the swimming pool, the Stepping Stones restaurant and recently, a new bistro, bothy and bar.

For this image Paul Tomkins goes west on the single-track road that follows the coast, where there's a historic farm and an ancient graveyard, Nunton Chapel and the wild beach at Culla Bay. On this quietly secret beach, here imbued with an almost melancholic atmosphere in the clear dying light, you can be sure of space for reflection.

PHOTOGRAPH **PAUL TOMKINS**

THE CORALBOX, BERNERAY

57°42'53"N, 7°10'15"W

Eilidh (and it seems to be just Eilidh) is the artist, owner and designer of the cutest shop in the Hebrides, a wooden box that, as a concept, began as a two-berth caravan when she returned to Berneray in 2015 after studying photography on the mainland and seeking a creative life in the place where she belonged.

As part of a project to portray key characters of the Hebridean community in their social and natural settings, John Maher meticulously positioned each subject in situ. This approach resonates with Eilidh's in her curation of the collection of crafts she keeps in the Box, stemming from her original photography, now embracing tasteful and useful stuff from soaps to stationery. There's no tartan and no mainland in sight.

The Coralbox is unmissable as you come into Borve, the main township, from the ferry a mile away.

PHOTOGRAPH **JOHN MAHER**

CASTLEBAY AND KISIMUL, EVENING

56°57′18″N, 7°29′10″W

Kisimul sits on a rocky outcrop 200 yards into the bay, guarding Castlebay and Barra, the last of the larger islands in the Hebridean archipelago. The ancestral home of the Macneils, you glide past on the ferry and immediately feel at home here. Built in the 11th century, burned out in the 18th and restored as recently as 1970, it is an essential pilgrimage for all Macneils and fascinating for all of us to visit, a forbidding exterior belying an intimate internal courtyard and rooms betwixt renovation and decay.

Jim Richardson's photograph reminds us in a poignant way that, even for this calendar-shot attraction and much-visited island, darkness does fall and everybody disappears. Perhaps they're at the top of this road that leads down to the quay in the famously convivial Irish kind of bar of the Castlebay Hotel, where the Vatersay Boys once presided over their legendary hoolies.

PHOTOGRAPH **JIM RICHARDSON**

MINGULAY

56°48'41"N, 7°38'21"W

In 1985, Derek Cooper wrote a book, *The Road to Mingulay*. It was a telling title, conjuring up a long journey to a romantic destination. It still intrigues and, for anyone trekking down the Hebrides, this would be, as it always was, the end of the road. Except, of course, you can only get there by boat and there will never be a causeway. Derek was in search of the place where his grandmother was born and, though in the 19th century 150 people scraped a living here, the last inhabitants left in 1912 and only sheep and birds will keep you company now.

Malcolm MacGregor also seeks out-of-the-way places and captures their remoteness and rawness in the photographs of his journeys to the edges and empty quarters of Oman, Namibia, the US and Scotland. On Mingulay there is nothing and nowhere to stay (though perhaps you can find shelter in the shell of the old schoolhouse) and no human artefacts except ruins like this: fragments of an abandoned Scotland.

PHOTOGRAPH **MALCOLM MACGREGOR**

THE ROAD

57°31'41"N, 7°10'58"W

This is The Road, the A865, that goes through North and South Uist and Benbecula, from near Berneray and the ferry to Harris in the north, by Lochmaddy and the ferry to Skye, and then to Lochboisdale in the south and the ferry to Oban. In the Uists you are never far from this road, from the sea and its fringing beaches. It is the spinal cord of the archipelago, the lifeline.

Paul's photograph was taken on Benbecula looking north to Grimsay. The hill is Eaval on North Uist.

Across skerries and remarkable causeways, sometimes like driving over the sea itself, the road is a feat of engineering. It could be the 'West Coast 100', but let's hope the marketeers don't get their hands on it. In the long open stretches, often with light traffic, it's a dream to drive or cycle. Going south in the late afternoon or evening, the sunset and the ocean all the way to America are on your right.

PHOTOGRAPH **PAUL TOMKINS**

THE MACHAIR

57°07'13"N, 7°23'30"W

The Machair (or Machar) is not a place, but a habitat – one of the rarest in Europe. A combination of a wet and windy climate, sand rich in shell fragments, and a gentle agronomy born of crofting culture, nourishes a unique carpet of grasses and flowers almost uniquely found in certain parts of northwest Scotland. North and South Uist are the best of places to experience it.

In summer the machair itself is a sea of delicate wild flowers and those from old crops like black oats and rye. It is also home to the great yellow bumblebee and the secretive corncrake. If you are lucky enough to hear the corncrake's distinctive *krek* call or see the swallows high in a wide blue sky, and the sea shimmering in the distance as you walk through a rippling field of flowers, and there's nobody around for miles, you know that...life is good. It is said that the scent of the machair, especially from the red clover, is strong enough for sailors to navigate by.

PHOTOGRAPH **DALZIEL**

VATERSAY

56°55′08″N, 7°32′14″W

This photograph by John Maher of the remains of a croft in the village of Uidh is not the usual image of Vatersay, which tends to show one of the remarkable crescent beaches on either side of the isthmus. Linked to Barra by a causeway built in 1991, the population has fluctuated since the Clearances from almost 300, after the resettling of people form Barra and Mingulay, to around 100 today.

After the First World War 'Pennyplan houses' were constructed by roofing in between the gables of abandoned crofts to encourage repopulation. Here the end walls, all that remains once again of an old dwelling, have been lit to 'put back light and life' into the ruins of what would have been the home of successive generations.

PHOTOGRAPH **JOHN MAHER**

NORTH AND SOUTH UIST AND BARRA: THE BEST OF

WHERE TO STAY

LANGASS LODGE, N UIST www.langasslodge.co.uk. 01876 580285. On the main road across N Uist, 5 miles S of Lochmaddy, the ferry port. Small hideaway hotel with rare garden and decent dining near Barpa Langass, a chambered cairn and important archaeological site, from 1000BC. There's also a good 2 mile waymarked walk. • HAMERSAY HOUSE, LOCHMADDY www.hamersayhouse.co.uk. 01876 500700. Contemporary recently refurbished hotel, same owners as Langass above. Best option to eat and sleep hereabouts. • POLOCHAR INN, S UIST www.pollacharinn.com 01878 700215. S of Lochboisdale, near Eriskay causeway and ferry to Barra. Makes most of its southern and western (sunset) aspect. Good rep for food and service. • ISLE OF BARRA BEACH HOTEL www.isleofbarrahotel.co.uk 01871 810383. A true beach hotel (Tangadale), 2 miles from Castlebay, meticulously run by the Jenkins/Adams family. Light public rooms, art, afternoon tea. Seals in the bay and sea to swim.

WHERE TO EAT

All above and • THE STEPPING STONE RESTAURANT, BENBECULA 01870 603377. Centre, near airport. Home-made food varying menu daytime and 6–8 pm. • CAFÉ KISIMUL, CASTLEBAY www.cafekisimul.co.uk. 01871 810645. By the quay, overlooking the castle and the bay, surprisingly good Indian (and some Italian) dishes restaurant. Lunch and dinner.

WHERE TO WALK

LOCHMADDY CIRCULAR: From Lochmaddy follow signs from the Outdoor Centre (and to the Hut of the Shadows), skirting the bay. 2 hour/4 mile walk is a good introduction to the waterscape: salt and freshwater lochans and islets in a European Marine Special Area of Conservation. • BARPA LANGASS AND LANGASS LODGE easy 1 hour walk (some places boggy) of both historical and topographical interest, with views. Starts on main road, follow signs. • BERNERAY: 4 hour loop of a fascinating island, starting at the Community Centre, mainly follows the coast, both townships and beaches. • HOWMORE (TOBHA MOR), S UIST. Easy ramble from turnoff on the main road, to historic church, thatched cottages, youth hostel and circular following beautiful beach. Machair and birds. • ERISKAY, consult locally and just walk. • BARRA: HEAVAL, the mini Matterhorn is steep but straightforward from Castlebay and straight up, past Our Lady of the Sea, sees you up. Less than 2 hours return.

SKYE

57°18′42″N,
6°12′11″W

SKYE

There are three ways to get to Skye, but still no airport – surprising considering that in 2019, 650,000 visitors arrived and it's a four-hour drive from Edinburgh. Perhaps that time has passed! There's the Bridge from Kyle of Lochalsh but the most memorable way to arrive is by the five-minute, community-operated Glenelg ferry to Kylerhea.

Skye is not only the biggest, most populous and most popular of Scotland's islands, it has more hotels, restaurants, campsites and hostels than the others put together. Still, somehow it has enough space to absorb everybody and, though certain sites are noticeably crowded, there's many a walk, scramble and climb (some seriously world-class) where you can take in enough scenery to appreciate what all the fuss is about. In Skye, it's the landscape that's the escape, which is why the photographs here show mainly the extraordinary topography; Skye must be the most photographed small island on Earth.

Much of Skye's accommodation is relatively expensive. Despite that, be advised to book well in advance. In the gazetteer at the end of this section, it's impossible to list many of those I'd recommend, so descriptions are brief. Also Eating Out. Perhaps a good thing about rising prices is that there's enough profitability to encourage investment, so every year there are more great places to choose from. I won't say much about attractions like Dunvegan, Talisker, Flora Macdonald's Grave or the Fairy Glen or Pools except that they attract lots of other people (see above).

That brings us to RAASAY (or the electric ferry does, from Sconser), surmounted by Dùn Caan with its unique truncated top, which you can see from Skye for miles. For me Raasay is the best little island of them all.

10 miles

10 kilometres

THE LITTLE MINCH

TARBERT, HARRIS

LOCHMADDY, NORTH UIST

Photo locations
1 Portree
2 The Bridge at Sligachan
3 On the Black Cuillin
4 The Lobster Man, Elgol
5 Isleornsay
6 Old Man of Storr
7 The Quiraing
8 Loch Slapin
9 Neist Point
10 Skye From Rassay
11 Dùn Caan from Skye
12 Raasay House

PORTREE
(PORT RIGH)

Scorrybreac

Scorrybreac Trail

Café Arriba

Loch Portree

Viewfield House

The Quiraing

7

UIG
(UIGE)

TROTTERNISH RIDGE

VATERNISH

Old Man of Storr

6

EDINBANE

RONA

The House Over-By at the Three Chimneys

DUNVEGAN

Skeabost

11

SOUND OF RAASAY

RAASAY

The Three Chimneys

9

Neist Point

1

PORTREE
(see inset)

SKYE
(AN T-EILEAN SGITHEANACH)

INNER SOUND

12 10

SCONSER

SCALPAY

KYLE OF LOCHALSH

CARBOST

MINGINISH

Oyster Shed

Sligachan Hotel

2

SLIGACHAN

KYLEAKIN

SEA OF THE HEBRIDES

CUILLIN HILLS

3

Loch Coruisk

BROADFORD
(AN T-ATH LEATHANN)

KYLERHEA
(CEOL REATHA)

Kinloch Lodge

8

Loch Slapin

Coruisk House

Duisdale House

ISLEORNSAY

ORNSAY

4

ELGOL

Hotel Eilean Iarmain

5

SOAY

Toravaig House

CUILLIN SOUND

ARMADALE

SOUND OF SLEAT

THE SMALL ISLES
(NA H-EILEANAN TARSAINN)
see page 232

MALLAIG

PORTREE

57°24'47"N, 6°11'40"W

You have a sense of how big this island is, driving/cycling here from the southern end and the Bridge. Portree is an increasingly thriving town with hotels, restaurants (including cheaper ones than elsewhere), a pool, galleries and shops and all the things you might need to stock up on for the hike or camp (including midge repellant). Downhill by the harbour, there's seafood cafés, the quayside commotion and the tang of the sea.

Portree is a base for the north of the island. Most of the places to explore are further north still via the road to Staffin, like the Old Man of Storr, seen here on the horizon or out west via Carbost and Edinbane. There are good roads on Skye but be prepared for single tracks and the slow caravanserai.

PHOTOGRAPH **PAUL TOMKINS**

THE BRIDGE AT SLIGACHAN

57°17'23"N, 6°10'24"W

For lovers of the outdoors, Sligachan is the historic junction of Skye. Climbers and walkers have passed through here for well over a 100 years. It's the gateway to Glen Sligachan, Glen Brittle and The Cuillin. Behind, and not in the photograph, rises the volcanic red cone of Glamaig (2543 ft). Every year runners race up its steep flanks, leaving from this bridge. Glen Sligachan divides the Red Cuillin from the Black, here seen in the distance.

On the other side, the Sligachan Hotel is a hostelry and haven going back to the misty early days of climbing and still run by scions of the family. Once an essential part of the Road to Skye experience – a statue by the bridge was erected (finally) in 2020 to the climbers who pioneered the Cuillin routes. The inn has moved with the times, its rooms, bar (and now brewery and beer garden) are a bustling road stop for a' folk: mountaineers and the rest of us.

Paul Tomkins drew my attention to the trailblazing travel writer (a pioneer himself), H. V. Morton. In his 1920's book *In Search of Scotland*, on arriving at the inn and waking up to see the sun rise over Glamaig and the clouds 'take fire above the jagged spires of the Cuillin', he further wrote 'I gasped, I literally lost my breath. No words can tell the strange atmosphere of this place, unlike anywhere else on earth.'

PHOTOGRAPH **PAUL TOMKINS**

ON THE BLACK CUILLIN

57°13'09"N, 6°14'18"W

The two Cuillin ranges separated by Glen Sligachan dominate the landscape of Skye. The iconic ridge of the Black Cuillin is all that remains of an eroded magma chamber of a giant volcano, its jagged edges sculpted by glacial activity and millennia of weathering. It is the UK's most challenging mountain range: eight miles long, with eleven Munros and 16 other summits. Blà Bheinn and Sgùrr Alasdair (the highest) are kings among many magnificent mountains.

Though the Cuillin can seem daunting, there are ways of experiencing it without risk or too much effort. Coire Lagan, a five-mile round trip from Glen Brittle, is a beautiful mountain loch surrounded by the highest peaks. Also on the four-mile walk around Loch Coruisk (by boat trip from Elgol), you are in an amphitheatre with one of the world's most spectacular backdrops.

Richard Cross's image from the heart of the Black Cuillin looks north towards Glen Drynoch across the ridge between Sgùrr Thuilm and Sgùrr a' Ghreadaidh. It was the first glimpse of sun on a filthy day. Richard and his companions had already climbed two peaks in the central ridge and were descending to Glen Brittle (the next day they conquered the infamous Inaccessible Pinnacle).

PHOTOGRAPH **RICHARD CROSS**

THE LOBSTER MAN, ELGOL

57°8'58"N, 6°5'54"W

The road to Elgol, the B8083 from Broadford, is one of the most worthwhile journeys to make in Skye: a good, mostly flat, though single-track, road round Loch Slapin in the shadow of mighty Blà Bheinn. When you come down the hill to Elgol past the superb Coruisk Lodge (hotel), Loch Scavaig with the backdrop of the Cuillin at its most resplendent, comes heart-stoppingly into view.

From the quay, boat trips (the *Bella Jane* or the *Misty Isle*) sail, as they have for generations, over the sea loch, with its whales, dolphins and basking sharks for the views of Soay island and Rum. They can drop you at the jetty for Loch Coruisk, made famous by Turner, and romanticized by Sir Walter Scott.

As well as big fish to Instagram, shellfish to eat have long been landed at Elgol Pier. Here is a man looking into Doug's camera, at home with his lobster fishing. It's done today much as it always was. One might imagine William and Walt having lobster for their tea.

PHOTOGRAPH **DOUGLAS CORRANCE**

ISLEORNSAY

57°8'51"N, 5°47'14"W

Isleornsay, though a white-cottage village overlooking the tiny island of Ornsay, is more thought of as a cove in a southern corner of Skye, with a hotel that makes the most of its ethereal location. Whether you arrive by boat to the old stone pier or by the short road off the main route through Sleat, you may feel that there is something almost mystic about this shore.

Once a busy herring port and then a stop for steamers from Glasgow, it's a quiet place now, except perhaps in the Praban pub, part of the Eilean Iarmain, the best hotel on Skye for *sui generis*, not to say generous Highland hospitality. There's a curated art gallery, a classy shop and a distillery. This is Skye at its most captivating (without the mountains).

PHOTOGRAPH **LUCILLA NOBLE**

OLD MAN OF STORR

57°14'58"N, 6°2'16"W

This spectacular pillar of basalt, the highest point of the splendid Trotternish Ridge, is eminently visible from the road north of Portree. On an island renowned for inspirational and challenging landscape, this is one of Skye's defining geological wonders. Easily accessible from the car park on the road, it's extraordinary from near or far, and impressive equally on a clear day or through Skye mist and squall: it is a photographer's dream.

PHOTOGRAPH **DAVID EUSTACE**

THE QUIRAING

57°38'21"N, 6°16'13"W

The Quiraing is simply phenomenal. In the far north of Skye, it's easily reached by the A855 from Portree, but the approach on the unclassified road from Uig reveals the full splendour more dramatically. The northern extension of the Trotternish Ridge, these contorted pillars and buttresses of eroded lava are as mysterious as they are astonishing. Gaze from the car park or walk around the 'Pillar', the 'Needle' and the 'Prison'. Fine views also to the island of Staffin and across the bay to Wester Ross.

PHOTOGRAPH **MARCUS MCADAM**

LOCH SLAPIN

57°11'29"N, 6°0'42"W

Loch Slapin is the four-mile-long sea loch that we circumnavigate
on the B8083 from Broadford to Elgol in the southwest of Skye.
Several Cuillin peaks jostle behind the loch, so it's an exceptionally
scenic drive or cycle. But Blà Bheinn, one of the most impressive and
easiest Munros to bag, dominates the sweeping cyclorama.
The most usual path to the summit (5 miles, 4 hours) starts at the
head of the loch from the John Muir car park.

This arresting yet serene and calming photograph was taken by
Jim Richardson in pre-dawn light.

PHOTOGRAPH **JIM RICHARDSON**

NEIST POINT

57°25'18"N, 6°47'12"W

Neist Point on the Duirinish Peninsula is west of Dunvegan, west of Carbost, west of everywhere else on Skye. This and the lighthouse make it a destination for walkers, wildlife watchers and photographers. Thrusting into the Minch, from here there are regular sightings of dolphins, porpoises, whales and basking sharks and, of course, seabirds on the cliffs.

The path to the lighthouse – built in 1900 and one of the most famous in Scotland – starts at the end of the single-track road from Glendale, seven miles from Dunvegan. On the 45-minute up and down walk, the lighthouse doesn't come into view immediately, but when it does it's a stately edifice, a worthy destination, as the field of stone cairns built by walkers, attests.

The Neist Point Lighthouse, like all lighthouses, is all about the sea. And as Julian Calverley's study reminds us – the sea is all about it and us, on our islands.

PHOTOGRAPH **JULIAN CALVERLEY**

FROM RAASAY

57°18'42"N, 6°12'11"W

This view from the hill above Raasay House at the bottom end of this small long island is one of the great outlooks of Skye. It is as if Raasay pays homage but keeps its distance. Clachan jetty at the foot of the grounds points to the seaway where we see the little ferry – Scotland's first electric ferry – coming across the Sound.

I have made that journey many times because to me Raasay is the perfect island. There's a great landmark hill (Dùn Caan) in the middle, woodlands and moorlands, a loch to swim in, a village (Inverarish) with rows of couthie cottages, a community shop and a new, quite flash distillery. Raasay's story is Scotland's history in microcosm. Some of that relates to the Big House, to the Clearances, to the now-famous Calum's Road and the iron mine, and to the huge range of outdoor activities that people now come here to engage in and to learn.

No apologies are made for the fact that in this book there are (disproportionately) three pictures of this one wee island, lying comfortably here in the sun, with Glamaig and the Cuillin, and big Skye over there.

PHOTOGRAPH **CAILEAN MACLEAN**

DÙN CAAN FROM SKYE

57°22'53"N, 6°1'45"W

The very distant hill in Cailean Maclean's image is Dùn Caan on Raasay, a hill to which I attach an almost spiritual significance. I'm not sure that anyone else does. However, its flat, serrated top, like a butte in the American West, is hugely distinctive as it stands in isolated splendour (at 443 m), quite apart from its blowhard big brothers in Skye. It's visible all the way up the road for miles on the A87 from Broadford to Sligachan. This picture was taken from the cleared village of old Skeabost in the middle of Skye. According to Cailean the celebrated Skye bard Màiri Mhòr nan Òran would have been able to see Dùn Caan from her window.

The walk to the hill requires a good hike into the wild heart of Raasay, usually starting at the Old Ironworks near the village. It's four/five hours there and back, but the panoramic view from the flat top, south to Skye and north across the nearby island of Rona to the mountains of Applecross, is exceptional. Johnson, or was it Boswell (and how intrepid were they?), said it was the best view in the Highlands. I would agree.

PHOTOGRAPH **CAILEAN MACLEAN**

RAASAY HOUSE

57°21'13"N, 6°4'45"W

Raasay House holds a lot of history from when it was torched by government troops after Culloden to when it was devastated by fire in 2009, weeks before a multi-million-pound refurbishment was about to be completed, gutting the whole building apart from the west wing. From Boswell and Johnson's visit in 1773 to the making of the *SAS: Who Dares Wins* TV show in 2019/21, and from becoming (after many opportunistic ownerships) the Scottish Adventure School in 1983 to the first-class Outside Activities Hotel/hostel/restaurant/bar it is today, this house is a Grand Survivor in itself.

Lyn Rowe, her daughter Freya and son-in-law David Croy picked themselves up after the fire and rebuilt the house back in its original layout and detail, from the insurance proceeds. Now it has comfy public rooms including a library, proper art on the walls and a programme of activities on land and sea, from archery to shooting the breeze up the hill. Out back is an exemplary community-run kitchen garden, it's a joy just to sit there. Behind is a marvellously evocative ruined chapel and in front the quay and a beach to swim from.

Did I say it was my kind of place? But staying here is an exemplary outdoor break experience for anybody and their kids.

PHOTOGRAPH **CAILEAN MACLEAN**

SKYE: THE BEST OF

WHERE TO STAY

HOTEL EILEAN IARMAIN, THE ISLEORNSAY HOTEL www.eileaniarmain.co.uk 01471 833332. Sleat, 15 mins S of Broadford. Gaelic coorie by the quay. Love the secret garden. • KINLOCH LODGE www.kinloch-lodge.co.uk 01471 833333. S of Broadford. Ancestral home of the Macdonalds. Top rooms, service and dining. • HOUSE OVER-BY at THE THREE CHIMNEYS, COLBOST www.threechimneys.co.uk 01470 511258. 4 miles W of Dunvegan. Few rooms, idyllic boutique, Michelin-starred restaurant, a true destination. • CORUISK HOUSE, ELGOL www.coruiskhouse.com. 01471 866330. 12 miles south from Broadford by stunning scenic road. Small, bespoke. Excellent dinner in conservatory. • DUISDALE HOUSE www.duisdale.com 01471 833202. TORAVAIG HOUSE www.skyehotel.co.uk 01471 833231. SKEABOST COUNTRY HOUSE www.skeabosthotel.com 01470 532202. Lovely v individual hotels. First 2 on Sleat S of Broadford, Skeabost nr Portree, locally owned SONAS COLLECTION. • SLIGACHAN HOTEL www.sligachan.co.uk. 01478 650204. Landmark, historic hotel with contemporary rooms. V outdoorsy. Big bar/bistro. Garden, brewery. • VIEWFIELD HOUSE www.viewfieldhouse.com 01478 612217. Just outside Portree. A long-time favourite, delightfully old-style. Less expensive than many. • RAASAY HOUSE www.raasay-house.co.uk 01478 660300. The big house on the wee island, rooms from luxe to bunks, beautiful outlook, garden and people.

WHERE TO EAT

All hotels above, fine dining in Kinloch and House Over-By. • SCORRYBREAC, PORTREE www.scorrybreac.com 01478 612069. Terraced house on road to Staffin. Few tables, much attention to Michelin fine fare. • LOCH BAY, STEIN www.lochbay-restaurant.co.uk. 01470 592235. Michelin-starred seafood in tiny restaurant in tiny Stein by the sea. Superb. • OYSTER SHED, Carbost behind Talisker Distillery. 01478 640383. Farm shop and seafood takeaway, oysters, lobster, crab. An outdoor adventure in food. • CAFÉ ARRIBA, PORTREE www.cafearriba.co.uk. 01478 611830. Upstairs on road to harbour. Long-established, laid-back boho café. Eclectic food.

WHERE TO WALK

SCORRYBRAC TRAIL. Easy shoreline walking on edge of Portree via road to Cuillin Hills Hotel. Good views, sea beside. Only 2 miles (or 4 via Storr Lochs). Can make circular going up over the hill, through woods back into town. • OLD MAN of STORR. The iconic 165-ft basalt finger seen from afar. Start at car park on Staffin road 20-ml N of Portree. Well-signed and -defined path. 2 mls. • THE QUIRAING. Scenic approach from Uig direction or Staffin road A855. The extraordinary rock pillars, 'The Table', 'The Needle', 'The Prison', easily approached. Take care going around, follow the others. Brilliant views. • THE TROTTERERNISH RIDGE. Many short or long walks around the 20 ml ridge in N Skye, can start going opposite direction from the Quiraing car park. Consult local guides.

MULL

56°26'24"N,
5°55'29"W

MULL

Mull is easy get to know, easy to love. There's a real town, Tobermory, with a picture-perfect waterfront, a wild heartland and long indented coastline, colonized by obliging wildlife. Alongside there are other diverse and fascinating islands: Ulva (for tranquillity), the Treshnish Islands (to hang out on with the puffins – one of Scotland's most intimate birdlife experiences) and Staffa for its renowned surreal geomorphology. Boat trips of long standing are well advertised.

Iona is simply unique. Let's face it, in Mull it does rain a bit, but Iona seems to have a benign microclimate of its own. God and St Columba may have something to do with that. Day trips don't get more rewarding than this, though it is a fair drive/bus/cycle to get to Fionnphort at the far southwest corner of Mull and hop on the ferry (no cars). There and back, a circular drive can take in scenic Loch na Keal and the coast of Loch Tuath to legendary Calgary Beach, passing Eas Fors, the waterfall that drops spectacularly into the sea (with wild swimming pools) on the way.

Mull is more geared up to visitors than most of the larger islands, its delights more accessible. There are some very good hotels and restaurants, mostly around Tobermory, and B&Bs, cottages and camping options aplenty. Have no regrets if you don't get enough of Mull and its offshore islands in a short sojourn, you'll probably be back.

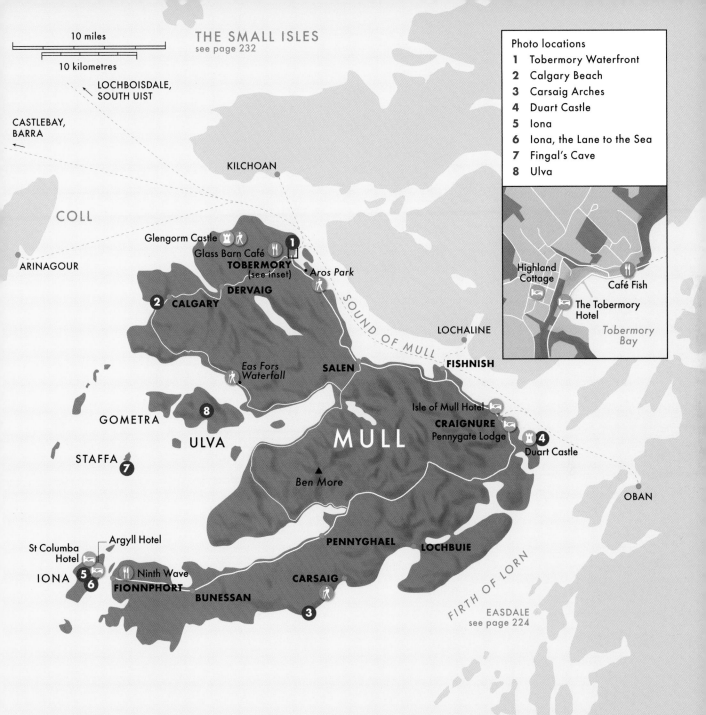

10 miles

10 kilometres

THE SMALL ISLES
see page 232

LOCHBOISDALE,
SOUTH UIST

CASTLEBAY,
BARRA

COLL

ARINAGOUR

KILCHOAN

Photo locations
1 Tobermory Waterfront
2 Calgary Beach
3 Carsaig Arches
4 Duart Castle
5 Iona
6 Iona, the Lane to the Sea
7 Fingal's Cave
8 Ulva

Highland
Cottage

Café Fish

The Tobermory
Hotel

*Tobermory
Bay*

Glengorm Castle
Glass Barn Café
TOBERMORY
(see inset)

1

• *Aros Park*

DERVAIG

2 **CALGARY**

SOUND OF MULL

LOCHALINE

FISHNISH

*Eas Fors
Waterfall*

SALEN

Isle of Mull Hotel

GOMETRA

8

ULVA

MULL

CRAIGNURE
Pennygate Lodge

4

Duart Castle

STAFFA

7

▲
Ben More

OBAN

PENNYGHAEL

LOCHBUIE

St Columba
Hotel

Argyll Hotel

Ninth Wave

IONA

5
6

FIONNPHORT

CARSAIG

BUNESSAN

3

FIRTH OF LORN

EASDALE
see page 224

TOBERMORY WATERFRONT

56°37′23″N, 6°3′57″W

The much-photographed 'colourful' waterfront of Tobermory Bay, epitomizing not only Mull but, often, the Southern Hebrides. A ferry leaves from here to Kilchoan on the Ardnamurchan Peninsula, a great way to go home, but most visitors from the mainland use the ferries arriving at Fishnish or Craignure (22 miles south). Tobermory has a very good sense of itself. The heart of the matter, the front, is like a promenade – there's even a fish 'n' chip van, aka the Fisherman's Pier. From here there are walks round the bay in both directions, and up the hill for great views and immaculate private cottage gardens.

In the photograph, the impressive landmark on the top right is the Western Isles Hotel. Below, on the dock, the white building is Café Fish. Run by two remarkable women, with Johnny's boat at the quay with the catch. We love Café Fish. Also on the front are the Mishnish and highly rated Tobermory Hotels and the estimable Tobermory Bakery (join the queue).

Hanging out in Tobermory is a pursuit in itself. Then there's an island to explore.

PHOTOGRAPH **ANGUS MCCOMISKEY**

CALGARY BEACH

56°34'40"N, 6°17'28"W

For many people memories of Mull are made of this. It wouldn't be too much of an exaggeration to describe Calgary Beach as legendary. And yet it's hard to put your finger on, or your toe in the water of why. You can swim, it's great to camp, there's a funky beach cabin (drinks and ice-cream), and the beach itself – it's treasured.

Doug's photograph was taken some years ago. It's still like this, except there's a lot more people. The car park and camping area by the road are quite a scene. Early-morning swims, sunset reveries, picnics and barbies make it feel like you're really on holiday, at a small festival in Australia. Somehow it's always clean and it's a happy vibe. That's perhaps why go.

Nearby is the Calgary Art Trail, a two-mile amble through woodland set out with sculpture and artworks. Start at Calgary Farmhouse where there's a gallery and café (check they're open); there's lots of self-catering accommodation around here.

PHOTOGRAPH **DOUGLAS CORRANCE**

CARSAIG ARCHES

56°17'35"N, 6°3'07"W

The Carsaig Arches are one of Mull's remarkable natural phenomena, and well worth the trek. Carved by erosion, they're part of a volcanic landscape at times supernatural. In the bottom southwest corner, you go off the main A849 for five miles to Carsaig Bay and start the four-mile walk at the pier. As you reach the first arch at the end of the track, descending from the ridge, it looks like an opening into the sea, or 'into another planet'. Other arches are like tunnels and there are sculpted pillars of basalt.

Sven Stroop aka Wojciech Kruczyński is a Polish photographer. 'Mystical landscapes' are his passion – 'the feelings that arise from contact with raw nature: delight, humility, admiration, sometimes ecstasy'. His work in his native Tatra Mountains and in Norway and Iceland is outstanding. Wild Scotland seems to be his other European home from home.

PHOTOGRAPH **SVEN STROOP**

DUART CASTLE

56°27′22″N, 5°39′18″W

Duart Castle, here seen from the sea, sits with immaculate strategic predominance at Duart Point, overlooking long Loch Linnhe, across the island of Lismore and all the way to Fort William. We go past Duart Point on the ferry from Oban.

Since the 13th century the ancestral seat of the Macleans, now home to Sir Lachlan and Lady Maclean, who make their visitors very welcome, Duart has weathered the storms of history and there's a lot of it on display. With walls as thick as a truck and on its isolated promontory, it was never much of a prospect to attack, but ruling over the unruly Macleans has been a proper job for centuries and nowadays the upkeep of the fiefdom has its own challenges. This is where you come in.

Duart is south of Craignure and a very decent half-day out, with sustenance at the airy 21st-century tearoom over the way.

PHOTOGRAPH **PAUL TOMKINS**

IONA

56°19'39"N, 6°24'32"W

Iona, the enchanted island, a place of pilgrimage for centuries, where an exiled Irish monk, St Columba, set up a community in AD 563 that became one of the most influential in Western Europe. Iona Abbey and the Iona Community remain ever active today and confer a spirituality to the place, tangible to all who come here. But it is perhaps a greater feeling of peace, a tranquillity that must always have been here, that makes Iona so compelling. Even the weather seems kinder than on Mull, from whence you've come; and it has a light that inspired the Scottish Colourists. People (around 150,000 a year) mostly come for the day, but it is magical to stay, climb the hill and wander as you will.

PHOTOGRAPH **DAVID LOMAX**

IONA, THE LANE TO THE SEA

56°19'51"N, 6°23'34"W

Iona for some folk means the Iona Community, the Christian fellowship centred (since 1938) at the Abbey, but there are people living here (over 100) going about their daily business. The post office and the ferry were once their only connections with the rest of the material world. Now there's the internet and (if we want) we're all connected, all the time. Not so long ago when this photograph by Paul Tomkins was taken, the boat bringing visitors (taking them away again at the end of the afternoon), the ferry dock and the post office were the social hubs.

This picture captures a time gone by but not gone away. The wonderful reassuring essence of Iona is that it can seem eternal.

PHOTOGRAPH **PAUL TOMKINS**

FINGAL'S CAVE

56°25'53"N, 6°20'29"W

This image couldn't really be anywhere else – instantly recognizable. Fingal's Cave, a sea cave on the uninhabited island of Staffa, about an hour's boat trip (from several points around Mull), has fascinated visitors since its discovery in 1772. Sir Walter Scott wrote that 'it exceeded in my mind every description I had ever heard of it' and the 20-year-old boy wonder, Mendelssohn was so moved by it when he arrived (seasick) in 1829 on the newly introduced paddle steamer service round Mull, that he was inspired to wrote his famed *Hebrides Overture*. The basalt columns, the huge arched entranceway and the cave's dimensions – 70 m deep, 23 m high – leave a profound impression. From the boat you get an hour or two to go inside and stroll the tiny island.

Jim Richardson is an American photographer whose work for *National Geographic* has brought him to Scotland on assignment (and because he loves it here) many times. On this occasion, staying at the Argyll Hotel, Iona he hooked up rather randomly with a couple of kitchen staff to help him set up and light the shot of the cave's otherwise dark interior and create this remarkable image.

PHOTOGRAPH **JIM RICHARDSON**

ULVA

56°28'48"N, 6°12'01"W

We were lucky with the glorious summer's day when we went to Ulva after lockdown in 2021. We swam in Ulva Bay, where the tiny ferry makes its five-minute crossing (you turn the board around to let the ferryman know you want to come over), we walked on pathways across woodland, hill and coast (Ulva is bigger than you think), saw the elegant Telford Church, looked into Sheila's Cottage, an interpretation centre, and had home-made food at the Boathouse by the quay. A perfect day!

In 2018, Ulva was the subject of a community buyout from its private owner, with help from the Scottish Land Fund. A manager was appointed to develop the estate appropriately and begin to repopulate the fragile community. Eight committed people live here now. It must be hard, but on a day like we had or one ending with a sunset like this, the idea of working from home in this brimming natural backyard and being part of a tiny purposeful community… well, it makes you think, as you head back to your mainland.

This image was taken by Les Gibbon of the British Wildlife Photography Award. Somebody took a picture of my friends with the ferryman and me, who had waited for us. We were the last visitors to leave.

PHOTOGRAPH **LES GIBBON**

MULL: THE BEST OF

WHERE TO STAY

THE TOBERMORY HOTEL www.thetobermoryhotel.com. 01688 302091. Middle of the bay; great outlook. Refurbished and contemporary, well-run bar with locals. Best restaurant on the waterfront. • **HIGHLAND COTTAGE** www.highlandcottage.co.uk. 01688 302030. Breadalbane St above the front. For a long time has been the best in town dining, and bespoke and delightful rooms (named after islands), conscientiously run by the Curries. • **PENNYGATE LODGE, CRAIGNURE** www.pennygatelodge.scot 01680 812333. 300 m from ferry, commanding views from a Georgian manor. Boutique rooms, contemporary menu serving the best dinner around. • **ISLE OF MULL HOTEL, CRAIGNURE** www.crerarhotels.com 01680 812544. Nr ferry (can pick you up). Most rooms on Mull. Spa and pool, decent dining. • **ARGYLL HOTEL, IONA** www.argyllhoteliona.co.uk 01681 700334. On the bay near the ferry and Abbey. Sympatico rooms and menu. Perfectly Iona, pray for a room. There's also the **ST COLUMBA HOTEL** www.stcolumba-hotel.co.uk 01681 700304.

WHERE TO EAT

CAFÉ FISH www.thecafefish.com 01688 301253. Simply one of the best seafood restaurants in Scotland, right on the quay, fish straight off the boat. Faultless ambience. • **NINTH WAVE** nr **FIONNPHORT** www.ninthwaverestaurant.co.uk 01681 700757. Far south, nr Iona ferry. Superlative fine dining but no airs. Carla Lamont's inspired cookery. • **GLASS BARN CAFÉ** www.isleofmullcheese.co.uk 01688 302627. The farm where they make the lauded IOM Cheddar (you can see it being made). Vintage barn with vines, big windows, terrace, garden. Nowhere like it and nobody like the Reades!

WHERE TO WALK

FROM CARSAIG: S on the Ross of Mull, starting at Carsaig Pier off the A849 nr Pennyghael. 2 Walks: 1. left towards Lochbuie spectacular coastal/woodland past Adnunan Stack (5 miles). 2. To the right, under the headland to the Nun's Cave and then 4 miles to Malcolm's Point and the remarkable Carsaig Arches carved by wind and sea. • **EAS FORS WATERFALL:** via Dervaig and Carsaig from Tobermory or from the south Salen and Loch Keal, a single-track road on a great coast. Signed and a pull-over car park, a stroll thro the woods uphill or the path down the grassy slope following the river to the sea. Short distances, but take care. • **EASY WALKS: GLENGORM CASTLE** from in front of the castle to the sea, where there's a natural swimming pool, and other walks in the estate. • **AROS PARK** S of Tobermory. The 'Art Trail' through the woods at Calgary Bay.

ISLAY

55°45'17"N,
6°13'02"W

ISLAY

Islay, gloriously understated in the Southern Hebrides, two hours from the Mull of Kintyre, offers a complete and unique island experience. A destination for whisky connoisseurs (tipplers, men of a certain age), birdwatchers and twitchers, golfers and walkers who don't need to climb mountains (though there are hills – seven Marilyns, hills above 150 m, Beinn Bheigeir being the highest) and history imbibers. It's easy to discover quiet beaches with different aspects and atmospheres. With magnificent Jura silently on the side via a five-minute ferry, there is a lot of contrast to absorb, but these islands can seep into the soul.

Between the two ports of Port Askaig and Port Ellen, a straight road takes you across the island through the main town Bowmore, the hub for all practical purposes: the Bowmore distillery, swimming baths, the unusual round church at the top of the hill and the Co-op. To the north from Bridgend, explore the Rhinns of Islay: the geese, the beaches – Machir and Saligo – and tranquil whitewashed villages. In the south from Port Ellen, the distilleries Laphroaig, Lagavulin and Ardbeg are all in a row on a picture-perfect coast. In the other direction, the wild Mull of Oa: the sombrely evocative American Monument and the locals', favourite beach, on the walk to the lighthouse, Carraig Fhada.

Islay and Jura: it's a rare blend.

10 miles

10 kilometres

COLONSAY

SCALASAIG

ORONSAY
see page 218

JURA

TAYVALLICH

SOUND OF JURA

9

LOCH
GRUINART

3 *Loch
Gruinart*

PORT ASKAIG

The Jura Hotel **CRAIGHOUSE**

SOUND OF ISLAY

Saligo Beach

Kilchoman Distillery **4**

Machir Beach

Islay House

Bruichladdich
Distillery

The Bridgend Hotel

KENNACRAIG

Peatzeria

BOWMORE

PORT CHARLOTTE

The Harbour
Inn

ISLAY

RINNS OF ISLAY

Port Charlotte
Hotel

5

Glenegedale House

PORTNAHAVEN

8

LOCH
INDAAL

*Laggan
Bay*

7

The Islay
Hotel

6

Ardbeg Distillery

Lagavulin Distillery

1

Laphroaig Distillery

**PORT
ELLEN**

2

Mull of Oa

Photo locations
1 Carraig Fhada Lighthouse
2 The American Monument
3 The Geese Arrive
4 Jura from Islay
5 The Big Strand
6 The Port Ellen Maltings
7 The Machrie Hotel
8 Portnahaven
9 The Paps of Jura

CARRAIG FHADA LIGHTHOUSE

55°37'13"N, 6°12'42"W

A great island should have a great lighthouse. This one, Carraig Fhada can't be missed as you arrive in Islay at Port Ellen, at the entrance to the harbour. It's unusually square and quite beautiful. The three-storey tower was built on the Carraig Fhada headland by the Laird of Islay in 1832 in memory of his wife, who died young at the age of 36. He also built Port Ellen. The lighthouse has no lantern, a signal light shines from a mast at the top and at sunset the whitewashed walls of the tower gleam. It's a landmark to be proud of.

Mark Unsworth is a professional photographer with a studio in Islay House Square near Bridgend where he shows and sells his work. Islay Square is home to other artists and the house itself is a hotel with woody grounds to walk in, and in summer a very pleasant outdoor café.

PHOTOGRAPH **MARK UNSWORTH**

THE AMERICAN MONUMENT

55°35'27"N, 6°20'01"W

On the southwest peninsula of the island known as Oa (pronounced Oh), six miles from Port Ellen, this impressive monument commemorates the shipwrecks nearby of two American troopships, the *Tuscania* and the *Otranto*. From a dramatic clifftop, the obelisk overlooks the sea, which is often beset by storms. This spectacular, though sometimes disquieting, place is a reminder of the tragedies, both in 1918 near the end of the war, one a U-boat attack, the other an accident. Together they were the greatest American loss of life since the Civil War. The monument was erected and is still managed by the American Red Cross.

To find it, take the road past the Port Ellen Maltings, marked Mull of Oa, for five miles. It is well signed, there's a car park and a mile walk, best done as a circular for fabulous island views.

Photographer Ben Shakespeare took this picture on the night the monument was lit to commemorate the centenary of the war on 11/11/2018. It is the only time it has been illuminated.

PHOTOGRAPH **BEN SHAKESPEARE**

THE GEESE ARRIVE

55°50'17"N, 6°20'08"W

Every October geese descend from the skies and reassemble in the fields of Islay, in the northwest around Loch Gruinart – 50,000 of them. Islay hosts about 60 per cent of the world's barnacle geese and a quarter of the threatened Greenland white-fronted geese. They clearly love it here, as do the simultaneously migrated birdwatchers – the farmers less so (though they receive some compensation). But this is a spectacular phenomenon, their epic journey putting Islay on the map as well as on their own. To some extent it is a symbiotic relationship.

George Robertson is also Lord George Robertson, the Labour politician who served as the tenth Secretary General of NATO from 1999 to 2004. A passionate Islay man, George is a keen photographer and has published two books that observe and document the island.

PHOTOGRAPH **GEORGE ROBERTSON**

JURA FROM ISLAY

55°58'50"N, 5°53'50"W

Jura is very close to Islay. The small ferry from Port Askaig in the north takes about five minutes. Mark's picture taken (with a telephoto lens), from a hill near Sunderland Farm and the Kilchoman Distillery on the west coast of Islay and actually about twelve miles away, shows how large it looms.

Jura, scarcely populated but occupying about half the landmass of Islay, has an ineffable grandeur, an almost unassailable integrity, though the Paps of Jura are one of Scotland's great island expeditions. A dram taken with or without the distillery tour at Kilchoman (where there's a great courtyard café) would set you up if you're looking for this vantage point, but the hotel bar at Craighouse supping the Jura on Jura is where you want to be.

PHOTOGRAPH **MARK UNSWORTH**

THE BIG STRAND

55°41'21"N, 6°16'28"W

The Big Strand, Islay's famously long seven-mile beach on Laggan Bay, on the west coast between Laggan Point and Kintra, faces the wild Atlantic foam and wind. It can make for a bracing stroll and in almost any weather the sunsets can be immense. Three rivers – the Laggan in the north and the Machrie and the Kintra – might impede progress walking end to end and, flanked by rolling, sometimes mountainous dunes, it's possible, even approaching from the golf course at The Machrie Hotel, to get lost.

You get a perspective on the Bigger Picture of the Big Strand coming in to land at the airport discreetly tucked away near the southern end, as we can also see in Jack Harding's photograph. Few places have a beach as special as this that is free from development. Long may we share in the sense of freedom it invokes.

PHOTOGAPH **JACK HARDING**

THE PORT ELLEN MALTINGS

55°38'03"N, 6°11'45"W

Islay is internationally renowned for whisky, those delectable peaty malts. The nine distilleries (there used to be more) are probably the main reason visitors come to Islay. Most of the distilleries are in settings, beautiful and romantic, satisfyingly commensurate with expectations. No wonder nearly all have popular tours, cafés and shops that make the most of their brand. There are probably more books about whisky and the historic and authentic premises it's made in, some lavish with photographs, than any other drink. So rather than choose from a rich gallery of options, favouring one barrel yard by the sea or atmospheric interior over another, this book pictures something more prosaic but nevertheless vital to all of them.

Ben Shakespeare was out one night on a mission to capture the full moon rising, but cloud came over. He was in Port Ellen and he noticed this, a shot he had to take: 'The Maltings', working late into the night, supplying the raw material for most of the Islay malts (Bowmore, Laphroaig and Kilchoman have their own malting floors). The barley (from elsewhere in Scotland and landed on the quay) is laid out to germinate, converting the starch to sugar for a week, then dried and mashed with peat. It's an organic timeless process, each distillery turning it into its own. The photograph seems to shield the secrets of an arcane alchemy.

PHOTOGRAPH **BEN SHAKESPEARE**

THE MACHRIE HOTEL

55°39'42"N, 6°15'02"W

The venerable Machrie Hotel and Golf Links has undergone a transformation in recent years, restoring both to pre-eminence (in hospitality and in the game).

The course, laid out across the links behind the sheltering dunes, was iconic from the start in 1891, and a complete redesign by architect D J Russell has opened up sea views, removed the notorious blind shots and added bunkers, so it's no longer maddening, just challenging good fun. In keeping with the opening up of the Machrie by new owners Gavyn Davies and Sue Nye, there's a more laid-back accessibility to the golfing experience: shop, golf tuition and a wee (six-hole) course.

The hotel also has significantly upped its game. Comfortable contemporary rooms, a great open dining room/restaurant with a balcony overlooking the greens. Lots of public space for locals and guests to meet and mingle. It's a stellar revitalized attraction for Scotland; Islay moving on up.

PHOTOGRAPH **JACK HARDING**

PORTNAHAVEN

55°40'51"N, 6°30'24"W

There is a surprising number of cute and thriving villages housing Islay's mere 3000-odd population. Bowmore and Port Ellen are busy wee touns, but up on the Rhinns, both Port Charlotte and Portnahaven seem to epitomize the island life: white-washed cottages looking out to sea.

Portnahaven is particularly pleasing to the eye and the sensibilities. The Rhinns of Islay lighthouse overlooks the village and the sheltered harbour. There's a cosy pub. Next door Port Wemyss is pure 'seaside' with calendar cottages. The villages share a church, once using separate doors. Of an evening exploring out west, come here and get to the Point.

PHOTOGRAPH **COLIN PALMER**

THE PAPS OF JURA

55°53'59"N, 6°01'02"W

For many of those who come again to cross the narrow Sound, Jura is in the blood. It's dominated by the Paps that we see from afar and we love it because of its wild emptiness and its self-contained island life. It gives solace.

A single-track road connects most of its 35 miles. Craighouse township has a great wee hotel – the social hub – with camping and a bar. There's a café, a shop and the distillery: the internationally revered Jura Malt. Every May, one of Scotland's most gruelling outdoor challenges – the Isle of Jura Fell Race – leaves the distillery and climbs the three Paps and four other tops, the winners back in just over three hours.

But we can take our time discovering Jura, a land that's always been uncompromisingly and powerfully itself.

PHOTOGRAPH **EUAN MYLES**

ISLAY: THE BEST OF

WHERE TO STAY

THE MACHRIE www.themachrie.com 01496 302310. The long-established now completely remade landmark hotel, in the centre of Islay by the airport, with a historic golf course on the dunes of the Big Strand. Trad values, contemporary dining, great friendly service and not so dear for de luxe. • **THE BRIDGEND HOTEL** www.bridgend-hotel.com 01496 810212. Near Bowmore at crossroads on the A846. Comfy, welcoming roadside hostelry. Owned and run by Islay Estates, lounge for tea, dining room on lovely garden, peaceful tasteful rooms. • **PORT CHARLOTTE HOTEL** www.portcharlottehotel.co.uk. 01496 850360. Inn on the shore of a quintessential island village. Good whisky (Bruichladdich distillery nearby), trad music. Good rep for food in bar and dining room. • **THE HARBOUR INN, BOWMORE** www.bowmore.com. 01496 810330. Harbourside inn with conservatory lounge and bar (with less formal supper). Contemporary rooms. Best bet in Bowmore. • **THE JURA HOTEL, CRAIGHOUSE** www.jurahotel.co.uk. 01496 820243. 12 km from the ferry at Feolin. The island hotel and pub and all-round social centre. Unpretentious accom with free camping by the sea. Beer garden. Near Jura distillery. • **THE ISLAY HOTEL, PORT ELLEN** www.theislayhotel.com 01496 300109. Very much part of the local community, bar and dining room with decent rooms on corner of the small town, gateway to the big distilleries. • **GLENEGEDALE HOUSE** nr **PORT ELLEN** www.glenegedaleguesthouse.co.uk 01496 300400. On the long straight A846 by the airport, a luxury guest house with rep for excellent dining, whisky and gin. Tasteful, homely comforts.

WHERE TO EAT

All of the hotels above are recommended. • **ARDBEG DISTILLERY CAFÉ** nr **PORT ELLEN** www.ardbeg.com 01496 302244. 5 km east of Port Ellen, pleasant walk or cycle. Good local and visitor reputation for daytime food. Gets busy. Home-made and all on brand. • **KILCHOMAN DISTILLERY CAFÉ** www.kilchomandistillery.com. 01496 850011. As above, essential as part of the whisky tour experience but popular with locals for daytime eats in restaurant or outside courtyard. The Cullen Skink is a winner. • **PEATZERIA, BOWMORE** www.peatzeria.com 01496 810810. Family-run Italian joint with surprisingly good pizzas. Bright café by the sea with mezzanine. The Islay alternative for eating out.

WHERE TO WALK

TO THE AMERICAN MONUMENT • On the Mull of Oa road from the Maltings building outside Port Ellen via Cragabus following signs for the monument. Car park. Walk 2 miles, return is easier than it looks. The circular allows clifftop views, farm animals (and wild goats). Monolith erected by the American Red Cross to commemorate 2 troop ships sunk 1918 in separate incidents off the Islay coast with unprecedented loss of life. An evocative place. • 3 Distilleries Walk (or amble) from Port Ellen past Laphroaig, Lagavulin and Ardbeg distilleries is easy, about 3.5 miles. Good café at Ardbeg. • Walks on/around Machir and Saligo Beaches both atmospheric and ever changing. Not safe to swim. Walks to the Carraig Fhada lighthouse and the Singing Sands near Port Ellen are easy; good for swimming. 5km. 2.5 hours. • Soldiers Rock and the Kintra circuit. Rocky coast (and sea stack), exhilarating though some boggy moorland. 5 miles. 3.5 hours.

ARRAN

55°33'46"N,
5°13'42"W

ARRAN

Arran is one of the most accessible and, as far as visitors are concerned, one of the most *comme il faut* of the Scottish Islands – especially for Glaswegians. With a frequent ferry service (albeit some issues in 2021), a de-stressing start to a holiday in itself, taking less than an hour, it has been the retreat and staycationing break of choice for generations of west coasters. With both a welcoming intimacy and an airy spaciousness, Arran is an easy place to fall in love with.

Distinctively different villages and communities – Lamlash, Whiting Bay, Lochranza, Corrie, Blackwaterfoot, and Brodick, where most people arrive – are spread out along their gentle bays.

The extensive Auchrannie Resort on the edge of Brodick is one of Scotland's best family and all-round hotels, almost a village of its own, and a hub for outdoor activities. Above it, above everything, Goatfell, just short of a Munro, is a proper mountain and a rewarding afternoon's exertion. There are sublime pristine beaches and walks and hikes of all standards, including a surprising mountain range with four Corbetts in the wilder interior. The Glens, Sannox and Rosa are easier ambles, as are the coast walk near Lochranza and to Glenashdale Falls by Whiting Bay. Brodick Castle and its wooded grounds is a lazier alternative.

When you think of Scottish Islands, don't forget about Arran, nearer than the misty Western Isles, small enough to find yourself, big enough to get lost in.

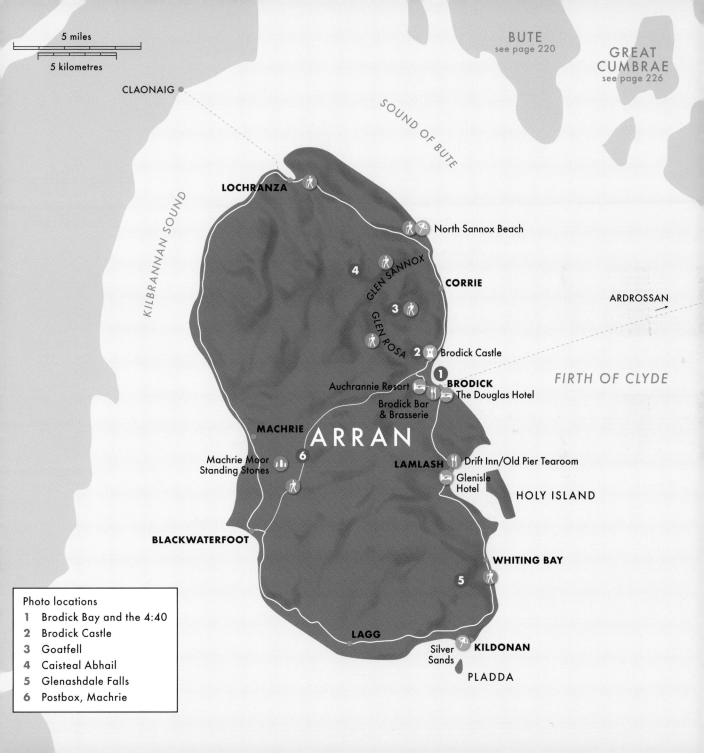

5 miles

5 kilometres

CLAONAIG

BUTE
see page 220

GREAT
CUMBRAE
see page 226

SOUND OF BUTE

KILBRANNAN SOUND

LOCHRANZA

North Sannox Beach

GLEN SANNOX

4

CORRIE

3

GLEN ROSA

2 Brodick Castle

ARDROSSAN

1 BRODICK

FIRTH OF CLYDE

Auchrannie Resort

The Douglas Hotel

Brodick Bar
& Brasserie

MACHRIE

ARRAN

6

Machrie Moor
Standing Stones

LAMLASH

Drift Inn/Old Pier Tearoom

Glenisle
Hotel

HOLY ISLAND

BLACKWATERFOOT

WHITING BAY

5

LAGG

KILDONAN

Silver
Sands

PLADDA

Photo locations
1 Brodick Bay and the 4:40
2 Brodick Castle
3 Goatfell
4 Caisteal Abhail
5 Glenashdale Falls
6 Postbox, Machrie

BRODICK BAY AND THE 4:40

55°35'07"N, 5°8'26"W

Brodick Bay is where most visitors to Arran arrive. This picture shows a wide swathe of the bay and nobody around. This is true sometimes, the bay has neither a marina nor a hoatching harbour, but when the ferry arrives or leaves, the quay is full of urgent comings and goings. It's amazing, when the ferry disgorges its passengers, how quickly they disperse around the island. In Arran, where the ferry service is crucial (hence much disgruntlement when it's delayed or cancelled), the timetable marks off the day. This one is 'The 4:40'.

Like all Arran's villages, Brodick is built along its long bay waterfront. It would take you half an hour to lug your luggage to the Auchrannie at the other end (there are taxis). You could be in Corrie or Whiting Bay on your bike by then, or putting up your tent in Glen Rosa. Nowhere is far away.

PHOTOGRAPH **ANDY SURRIDGE**

BRODICK CASTLE

55°35'38"N, 5°9'03"W

Round the bay and up the coast road is Brodick Castle, not a castle in the fortified battlements sense of the word, but a big old baronial pile of history, 'quintessential' says the National Trust. From some angles, it's a substantial edifice, from others as here, it's more like a tower house. Originally from the 13th century and, until the 1950s, the home of the Dukes of Hamilton, there are both stately and more liveable rooms, with antlers, portraits, heirlooms and an atmosphere of long-ago afternoons.

The extensive grounds of Brodick Castle, open all year, are a treat, ranging from formal gardens recently restored perhaps even beyond their former glory, to forest trails and wilder bits, where you feel the presence of Goatfell, also in the NTS domain. Rhododendrons are big and pink in spring, in autumn it's a riot of golden autumn colours. Often you see the sea through the trees, reminding you you're on an island and these woodlands are part of the rich diverse natural playground that is Arran.

PHOTOGRAPH **ANDY SURRIDGE**

GOATFELL

55°37'33"N, 5°11'31"W

On Arran, Goatfell presides. It's there when you arrive, there when you leave. If you're fit, it will remind you all the time that it's just waiting to be climbed.

At 874 m, it's just short of a Munro, but is one of four Corbetts on the island. The usual start is by the Arran Brewery and Wineport pub two miles from town on the road to Corrie. There's another start further up that road, near Sannox. Coming back that way might suggest a dip in the sea at the beach at North Sannox. Allow four to five hours for Goatfell. A scramble at the top, but needless to say, there are topping views. The beach here is one of several that are great for families.

PHOTOGRAPH **JOE DUNCKLEY**

CAISTEAL ABHAIL

55°38'58"N, 5°13'49"W

This image, which conveys how mountainous Arran actually is, shows Goatfell from an unfamiliar perspective, along with other Corbetts (hills between 2500 and 3000 feet). Richard Cross, starting from Glen Rosa, climbed to the summit of Caisteal Abhail, aka the Sleeping Warrior – you can see him and his friends faintly over there – and sent up a drone. The result is a unique photograph of a mountain ridge that most of us have never noticed.

The Corbetts here, Cìr Mhòr, Goatfell and Caisteal Abhail, together with Beinn Tarsuinn (to the right of the picture), can all be bagged in a twelve-mile ten-hour expedition. You'd want it to be a day like this one. There are 217 other Corbetts in Scotland and 282 Munros.

PHOTOGRAPH **RICHARD CROSS**

GLENASHDALE FALLS

55°28'44"N, 5°7'11"W

The walk to Glenashdale Falls is one of the great natural jaunts of Arran. It's within most physical capabilities, but with enough effort and concentration required to give a sense of achievement, you reach a destination that doesn't disappoint. It can be a circular walk but the usual start is signed by the Glenashdale Bridge on Whiting Bay's main road. You follow the river along its course and gorge, through woodland (some tracts have been cleared) on a path where staircases ease progress on the steeper bits. There are viewing platforms across from and above the Falls and places to stop and picnic, perhaps on the sausage rolls, pies and cakes you may have bought from the estimable Old Pier Tearoom and Bakery in Lamlash.

The circular, less defined track, back down the other side, swerves through pine woods and you emerge past the golf course on the road in Whiting Bay again beside the Coffee Pot (and more excellent home baking). This is not a survival course in the great outdoors, more like a country walk with rewards.

PHOTOGRAPH **ANDY SURRIDGE**

POSTBOX, MACHRIE

55°33'20"N, 5°16'49"W

The Postbox has always been an important fixture on an island where, as in many rural places, it might be a long way to the town and the post office and connection with the rest of the world. The post van brings the letters and the parcels back from the family gone away (and the latest local gossip). The postbox in the middle of the nowhere, where you live, is how you reply, how you keep in touch.

All changed by the internet, Amazon, deliveries of everything, even to far-flung parts, there are still those who write a letter, send a card for a birthday or Christmas. This postbox still here on the 'String Road' between Brodick and Blackwaterfoot, near the Machrie Moor Standing Stones, may seem like a nostalgic anachronism, a postcard of bygone days but, after it was knocked over in an accident, they were right to build it back. It's almost like a piece of living sculpture. A myriad of letters, pages of real-life stories will have been pushed through the slot, and been passed on.

PHOTOGRAPH **DOUGLAS CORRANCE**

ARRAN: THE BEST OF

WHERE TO STAY

AUCHRANNIE RESORT www.auchrannie.co.uk 01770 302234. A locally run, well-managed holiday complex: the old mansion, the newer block (both have restaurants and pools) and lodges. 10-min walk into Brodick. Programme of activities indoors and out. • **THE DOUGLAS HOTEL** www.thedouglashotel.co.uk. 01771 302968. Hotel by the pier in Brodick. Local ownership, food, art. Dining room, bistro and bar. • **GLENISLE HOTEL** www.glenislehotel.com. 01770 600559. On Lamlash bay looking over to Holy Island. Modern hotel and inn, restaurant with rep, bar with bayside garden.

WHERE TO EAT

All hotels as above. Auchrannie has finer dining Eighteen69, Brambles Bistro and family restaurant Cruize. All good. The Douglas IS Arran. • **BRODICK BAR & BRASSERIE** 01770 302169. Off N end of main road. Best restaurant food in town. Friendly service, some imaginative cookery. Must book. • **THE DRIFT INN, LAMLASH** www.driftinnarran.com. 01770 600608. Off main road making most of its seaside location with terrace and garden. Good pub and grub. • **OLD PIER TEAROOM, LAMLASH** 01770 600249. Tearoom/café and takeaway on lane to quay for boat trips to Holy Island. Chris Davis's outstanding home baking.

WHERE TO WALK

GOATFELL. The hill must be climbed (if you're reasonably fit). Starts at Arran Brewery, 2 mls N of Brodick or N of Corrie. 874 m. Famously rewarding. • **GLENASHDALE FALLS, WHITING BAY.** Superb 3 ml walk following gorge from main st at bridge, circular via the golf club. A climb with staircases, not arduous. • **MACHRIE MOOR STANDING STONES.** By B880 Brodick to Blackwaterfoot (4 mls) or coast rd. Circles, stones, cairns, a notable archaeological site. 2.75 ml walk, flat moorland. • **GLEN SANNOX** and **GLEN ROSA.** Glens N and W of Brodick. Car parks and walks marked. **GLEN ROSA** has a brilliant wild campsite and **THE BLUE POOL** for swimming. **NORTH SANNOX BEACH** is so good. SILVER SANDS sublime – S of Whiting Bay, 500 m off A841 signed Kildonan. • **COCK OF ARRAN COASTAL WALK.** From Lochranza Golf Course, follow road round coast to last houses and keep going all the way to Sannox (10 mls, or any part of it). Shorter and circular, after half mile, turn up hill path at the house on the beach where main path peters out, along the cliffs back to Lochranza (2 mls).

ORKNEY

59°3'24"N,
2°56'31"W

ORKNEY

Orkney isn't just a group of islands, it can feel like another country. It has its own flag and a distinctive dialect of Scots (very pleasing to the ear) and many unique words. The islands were colonized and annexed to Norway in the ninth century until the 15th, when they became part of the kingdom of Scotland; the Norse influence is evident. Inhabited for 8500 years, Orkney contains some of the oldest and best preserved Neolithic sites in Europe. Those like Skara Brae, the Stones of Stenness and the structures at the Knap of Howar on Papa Westray (the latter more than 5000 years old) are astonishing and part of an extensive UNESCO World Heritage Site.

The other major historical impact was more recent. Over two World Wars, Orkney, with its strategic position in the North Sea and the significance of sheltered Scapa Flow, became a huge base for the Royal Navy. The sunken remnants of the infamous scuttling of the sequestered German High Seas fleet in 1918 can still be seen, and the 'Churchill Barriers. The affecting Italian Chapel, south of Kirkwall, by Burray, is simply extraordinary.

There are ferries overnight from Aberdeen, or much shorter journeys from the north coast at John o' Groats (seasonal) and Scrabster. Loganair fly to Kirkwall from Edinburgh, Glasgow, Aberdeen and Inverness. There are 70 islands in the archipelago, 20 inhabited, the larger with services run by Orkney Ferries. To get Orkney, you should go exploring, not only to Hoy for the Old Man and the beach and cliffs at Rackwick or to the Westrays, but to the other islands – too many to draw attention to here. Read up, ask. And plan ahead.

VISIT ORKNEY: 01856 872856
NORTHLINK FERRIES: www.northlinkferries.co.uk 0800 111 4422
PENTLAND FERRIES: www.pentlandferries.co.uk 01856 831226
ORKNEY FERRIES: www.orkneyferries.co.uk 01856 872044

ORKNEY ISLANDS

ATLANTIC OCEAN

10 miles

10 kilometres

WESTRAY FIRTH

WESTRAY

PAPA WESTRAY

8

5

THE NORTH SOUND

NORTH RONALDSAY

9

LERWICK, SHETLAND

SANDAY

SANDAY SOUND

ROUSAY

EGILSAY

10

EDAY

STRONSAY

Brough Head

11

BIRSAY

Marwick Head

Birsay Bay Tearoom

MAINLAND

FINSTOWN

STRONSAY FIRTH

SHAPINSAY

YESNABY

12

3

KIRKWALL (see inset)

The Kirk Gallery and Café

1 2

Julia's Café Bistro

STROMNESS

The Foveran

Kirkwall Airport

SKAILL

GRAEMSAY

HOUTON

Moaness Pier

SCAPA FLOW

4

FLOTTA

7

HOY

Churchill Barriers

BURRAY

LYNESS

6

ST. MARGARET'S HOPE

SOUTH RONALDSAY

BURWICK

PENTLAND FIRTH

ABERDEEN

NORTH SEA

SCRABSTER

JOHN O'GROATS

Duncansby Head

KIRKWALL

The Storehouse

Real Food @ Judith Glue Café

Lucano

Lynnfield

Highland Park Distillery

Photo locations

1 Stromness
2 The Pier Art Centre, Stromness
3 Standing Stones of Stenness
4 The Old Man of Hoy
5 Going to the Spoots
6 Stanger Signal Station
7 The Italian Chapel
8 Pierowall
9 North Ronaldsay
10 St Magnus, Egilsay
11 The Brough of Birsay
12 Sun on the Cliffs at Yesnaby

STROMNESS

58°57'48"N, 3°17'51"W

Stromness in the west is the other town on Mainland Orkney. Kirkwall is the capital and civic centre: the airport, the hospital, the harbour, St Magnus Cathedral and the Highland Park whisky distillery. In the main street are some surprisingly up-market and interesting shops. Stromness offers something less tangible: a spirit, a cultural connection; seaworthiness.

Jim Richardson's aerial image shows a couthie small town on its cape, surrounded by verdant green farms, like much of Orkney, facing across to Hoy and the small island of Graemsay – facing the world. Obviously the sea has shaped the history of the settlement that the Vikings called Hamnavoe (haven in the bay). Fishing flourished in the abundant but perilous waters of the Pentland Firth, as did shipbuilding and whaling (the men who crossed to the Hudson's Bay Company returned the richer). Stromness, with its alleyways, braes and unexpected piers, seems like a place apart, somewhere in Northern Europe, perhaps where once it traded with the Baltic ports (and as far as the American colonies).

Stromness is a quieter, more reflective place now. Ferries arrive from the north coast of Scotland, smaller boats from Hoy. Folk disembark and seem quickly to be absorbed into the stone streets. Not gentrified, effortlessly authentic, it's one of the most atmospheric towns in Scotland. Go quietly.

PHOTOGRAPH **JIM RICHARDSON**

THE PIER ART CENTRE, STROMNESS

58°57'46"N, 3°17'53"W

On a landing between the main street and the sea, the Pier Art Centre is a fascinating, uniquely important art gallery. It houses the collection of Margaret Gardiner (1904–2005), regarded as one of the finest collectors of contemporary 20th-century British art; it is partnered with the Tate. Gardiner knew many of the artists, Barbara Hepworth, Ben Nicholson and Stanley Cursiter, personally. More recent acquisitions – Sean Scully, Olafur Eliasson, and also in the permanent collection, notable contemporary Scots: Martin Boyce, Douglas Gordon and Callum Innes – offer an impressively curated and surprising exposure to good modern art.

Howell also kept company with other luminaries and writers of the period, and was a close friend of the internationally revered writer, George Mackay Brown, for whom Stromness, his birthplace, was a lifelong inspiration. His many books, including his memoir, *For the Islands I Sing*, are on sale in the gallery bookshop. At the Pier you board a boat for an enlightening journey.

PHOTOGRAPH **ALISTAIR PEEBLES**

STANDING STONES OF STENNESS

58°59'39"N, 3°12'29"W

Orkney Mainland is rich in prehistory. The Stones of Stenness stand just off the Kirkwall to Stromness A965, on the road that also leads to the Ring of Brodgar and Skara Brae. Maes Howe, a pre-eminent chambered cairn, is nearby. Together these four sites constitute Orkney's outstanding and easily accessible World Heritage Site.

Skara Brae is the prize, one of the best conserved prehistoric sites in the world. As the excellent Visitor Centre explains, the compact shoreline village of 5000 years ago was engulfed in a sandstorm six centuries later and lay preserved until discovered by the Laird's foraging dog in 1850. We know now how they/we lived back then, what they ate and, as you walk around the raised embankments looking down into the stone houses, it is a uniquely thought-provoking glimpse of life an inconceivably long time ago.

To my mind, the Stones of Stenness (three of the four, originally twelve, are shown here) are the most aesthetic of the ancient monoliths, elegant and particularly enigmatic as the sun goes down.

PHOTOGRAPH **PAUL TOMKINS**

THE OLD MAN OF HOY

58°53'11"N, 3°25'50"W

Famous is the Old Man of Hoy, like Scotland's other old men, Stoer and Storr. We want to go and meet them or even climb up them. At 449 ft, this Old Red Sandstone sea stack hit the news when it was conquered by Chris Bonnington in 1966. But the Old Man is only part of the reason many come across to Hoy (from Stromness preferably, or Houton). Hoy is where the big scenery is, the hills reminiscent of Highland Scotland. You cross the island by bike or bus (from Moaness which meets the Stromness ferry). On foot from Moaness is a hike (14 miles). There's a welcome café there however you come or go, near the ferry.

The bus (public, or private minibus) takes you to Rackwick, where the Old Man of Hoy walk (6.5 miles, 3 hours) begins, but it would be a pity not to allow time to walk on, or swim from, Rackwick Beach, its headland rising massively above.

Rebecca's photograph is unusual because it reminds us that the Old Man, peeping over, stands apart among many other sheer and magnificent cliffs. And we can appreciate what a challenge and a feat it is to cross the channel and climb it.

PHOTOGRAPH **REBECCA MARR**

GOING TO THE SPOOTS

59°19'50"N, 2°53'45"W

'Spoots' is a good old Scots word for razor clams. It comes from the spout of water the mollusc makes when it burrows into the sand. In Orkney you don't collect or gather them, you 'go to them' at low tide, as if they were waiting for you.

Rebecca Marr's image is of her friends walking the strand on Papa Westray, aka 'Papay', at the spring tide. Spotting and foraging for spoots seems a good and purposeful way to spend a day at the beach. Although Rebecca, for one, confesses not to be a connoisseur (there's a bit of messy prep), plenty of garlic renders the humble razor clam a rare and pure organic treat.

PHOTOGRAPH **REBECCA MARR**

STANGER SIGNAL STATION

58°48'58"N, 3°5'11"W

On the island of Flotta there is an indelible imprint of the Wars. Scapa Flow was a huge sheltered anchorage for the Royal Navy, which had to be serviced and protected. When you go there today (by ferry from Houton), perhaps to walk on the quiet roads and pathways of Flotta, leaving the busy Oil Terminal quickly behind, it's hard to imagine there were once 10,000 to 20,000 servicemen (and a few women) here. The museum at Lyness, just across the Sound on Hoy, and the Flotta Heritage Centre tell the story well, but the island itself is a living interactive museum, where the echo of those tumultuous years can still be heard.

The strategically situated Port War Signal Station at Stanger Point had a crucial communications role to play. In Rebecca Marr's photograph we are looking across a water-filled quarry at a long-abandoned building, stark in black and white like a photograph from back then. Actually the Signal Station was a complex of buildings looking over the other side of the ridge out to sea. This is the tower, but the image captures a relic forlorn, a war long gone, practically forgotten, the gulls still dipping in the water.

PHOTOGRAPH **REBECCA MARR**

THE ITALIAN CHAPEL

58°53'24"N, 2°53'22"W

Many of the remnants of the Great Wars in Orkney are evocative and have an air of melancholy, of abiding interest, mainly for followers of naval history and nostalgia enthusiasts. The Italian Chapel, near the first Causeway and Churchill Barrier on the A961, six miles south of Kirkwall, is different. It's inspirational.

In 1943, Italian POWs captured in North Africa and transported here to Lamb Holm in Orkney were given permission by the Camp Commander to transform two Nissen huts into a place of worship. Using the most meagre materials, they created a remarkably ornate chapel, completed at the end of the war in 1945. The meticulous trompe l'oeil and wrought-iron work, a team effort led by Domenico Chiocchetti, remain to this day, a deeply affecting affirmation of faith.

The Chapel, restored in the 1960s and again in the 1990s, has become one of Orkney's tourist attractions. Domenico returned after the war, an honorary Orcadian.

PHOTOGRAPH **DOUGLAS CORRANCE**

PIEROWALL

59°19'11"N, 2°59'25"W

Westray and Papa Westray are islands to the north of Mainland Orkney. Ferries go between them and to Kirkwall, or you can get there on a very special flight: the 15-minute trip to Westray and then the two-minute flight to Papay (as it's known locally) are the shortest scheduled flights in the world. Jim's image of Pierowall, the main township, was taken not by a drone but from a plane. It shows its beautiful circular natural bay and harbour from a revealing aerial perspective.

On Papay you find yourself in a small green patch of island heaven with a handful of people and a skyful of birds. The clifftop walk at Noup Head on Westray gives you a look-over into one of the seabird cities of the north. It's less than five miles there and back to the especially fine lighthouse from Backarass Farm, a mile from Pierowall.

PHOTOGRAPH **JIM RICHARDSON**

NORTH RONALDSAY

59°22'21"N, 2°25'18"W

North Ronaldsay, the farthest north of the North Isles and the farthest away from Kirkwall and mainland Scotland, is home to 60 people. Jim Richardson's study focuses on the boat – a praam (or pram), designed and built only here. Copied from a boat being transported by a Norwegian ship passing by in 1926, this sturdy unique wooden fishing boat was adapted to account for North Ronaldsay's skerry-lined coast and steep beaches. The one here had been lobster fishing. There are few praams left now, though one, *Pearl*, has been recently restored.

At 139 ft, the Dennis Head Lighthouse is the highest land-based lighthouse in the UK. North Ronaldsay also has its own eponymous breed of sheep. Not bad for an island where 'remote' doesn't quite cover it, to have its own boat and its own animal. Edge lovers – you should get out here.

PHOTOGRAPH **JIM RICHARDSON**

ST MAGNUS, EGILSAY

59°9'25"N, 2°56'07"W

Tiny Egilsay, east of larger Rousay, is known for this, the church of St Magnus, who was killed on the island way back in 1117 by an axe blow to the head. St Magnus was central to all things religious on Orkney. His much more famous and suitably magnificent church is in Kirkwall: St Magnus Cathedral.

In the photograph the ancient church, its bell tower (once seen and heard for miles) and graveyard sit in a tablecloth of green farmland, like a reliquary of centuries of living on the land and thanking God for all things. Fewer than 20 souls live on Egilsay today. And the endangered corncrakes most partial to the peace and quiet.

PHOTOGRAPH **JIM RICHARDSON**

THE BROUGH OF BIRSAY

59°8'11"N, 3°20'06"W

At the northwest Point of Orkney Mainland in Birsay Bay, the Brough is a low-lying island joined to the mainland by a tidal causeway that you can cross only two hours either side of low tide. This makes for a slightly edgy walk because, if the tide races in, you could be stuck for eight hours – obviously there's no pub, only a lighthouse and a few thousand seabirds. The views and the sunset can be epic, though, and the walk is one of the most popular sections of the West Coast Walk. From Birsay Village it's two hours return. There is a proper path, which you can see in Ingrid Budge's photograph, going up the Brough on the either side. In Birsay are the ruins of the Earl's Palace, a 16th-century courtyard castle. The estimable Birsay Tearoom is nearby.

Ingrid Budge has a shop and gallery of her work in Albert Street, Kirkwall, near the Cathedral.

PHOTOGRAPH **INGRID BUDGE**

SUN ON THE CLIFFS AT YESNABY

59°1'29"N, 3°21'31"W

The red cliffs of Yesnaby are to Orkney what the white cliffs are to Dover and England. Somehow they're emblematic; folk say, with a wistful sigh, you must at least go there before you leave. Here the sun is on them in the late afternoon.

The red colouration is because the cliffs are of Old Red Sandstone, from which the sea has carved blowholes, geos and sea stacks. One of them, 'Yesnaby Castle', is popular with climbers, a mini Old Man. Part of the West Coast Walk, south of Skara Brae, Yesnaby is off the A967, seven miles north of Stromness.

You must go there too.

PHOTOGRAPH **INGRID BUDGE**

ORKNEY: THE BEST OF

WHERE TO STAY

THE STOREHOUSE, KIRKWALL www.thestorehouserestaurantwithrooms.co.uk. 01856 252250. Smartest stay in town, contemporary restaurant/bar on ground floor of remade listed building in lane behind the Cathedral, 8 cool rooms above. • **LYNNFIELD, KIRKWALL** www.lynnfield.co.uk. 01856 872505. 10 mins from downtown next to Highland Park Distillery. V comfortable trad rooms and superlative dining. • **THE FOVERAN** www.thefoveran.com. 01856 872389. 3 miles W of Kirkwall overlooking Scapa Flow. Delightful family-run country hotel, decent rooms, excellent dining with the view.

WHERE TO EAT

Best eating out in Kirkwall at the Lynnfield, outside town at the Foveran (above). Locals know this, you should book. • **THE LEONARDS @THE STOREHOUSE** 01856 252250, as above • **REAL FOOD @ JUDITH GLUE CAFÉ**, KIRKWALL www.judithglue.com. 01856 874225. Main St opposite Cathedral, long-established craft/gift shop and self-service café, home made real food, same folk as The Storehouse above. • **LUCANO, KIRKWALL** www.lucanokirkwall.co.uk 01856 875687. Old-style family-run Italian, all the faves. Best restaurant in town centre. • **BIRSAY BAY TEAROOM** www.birsaybaytearoom.co.uk. 01856 721399. N of Mainland, 30 mins Kirkwall nr The Earl's Palace and Marwick Head, Brough walks. Home bakes, home-grown. • **JULIA'S CAFÉ BISTRO, STROMNESS** www.juliascafe.co.uk 01856 850484. Opposite the ferry terminal nr harbour. Local café with home bakes and filling fare. • **KIRK GALLERY AND CAFÉ, TANKERNESS** www.sheilafleet.com. 01856 861203. 5 mls from Kirkwall nr airport. Impressive showrooms of Sheila Fleet's jewellery and excellent restaurant for daytime home-made, locally sourced delicious food.

WHERE TO WALK

Difficult, i.e. impossible, to select 'best walks' from the endless options on a dozen accessible islands. All across The Mainland from South Ronaldsay to Brough Head and from the islands of Hoy and Flotta to North Ronaldsay, there are bracing coastal walks and historic places to discover. And hardly any hills (or trees). However, don't miss: • **HOY**. A dramatic coastline (and a rare mountainous interior) includes **THE OLD MAN OF HOY** and close by, fabulous **RACKWICK BEACH** and headland. Ferry from Stromness to N end at Moaness, then by bus 4 mls across Hoy to Rackwick. Or to S of Hoy at LYNESS and the Scapa Flow (war) Museum, then bus or drive/cycle N. The ferries (from Houton) also go to FLOTTA: much war nostalgia; less known but fine walking. • **MARWICK HEAD** and **BROUGH HEAD**. N Mainland, 30 mins Stromness, 40 mins Kirkwall. Part of the 7-mile West Coast Walk where sections include • **THE YESNABY CLIFFS, THE BAY OF SKAILL** (and the world-class **SKARA BRAE** Neolithic site), then N to **MARWICK HEAD**. All sites have exceptional clifftop views and important seabird colonies.

SHETLAND

60°20'32"N,
1°13'44"W

SHETLAND

Shetland is sometimes described as the destination for people who want to find somewhere genuinely unspoilt. If by unspoilt we also mean underdeveloped (and despite Sullom Voe, one of the largest oil terminals in Europe), this would be true of this bountiful island archipelago stretching far into the north. Shetland, fiercely independent and self-reliant (even of tourism) has not gone the way of other islands and themed or schemed its landscape, history and culture to suit the perceived predilections of visitors.

Unquestionably, a factor in keeping its distance (and integrity) is that it is 110 miles from mainland Scotland, 800 miles from London, and 12 hours on the ferry from Aberdeen. Fishing and, since the 1970s, the oil and gas industry have been the economic drivers and 'tourist attractions'. 'Restaurant culture' and bespoke hotels have not emerged (or blotted the landscape). The Shetland Folk Festival, celebrating its 40th anniversary in 2022 and Up Helly Aa (hard to get a room anyway), two of the most authentic and best cultural get-togethers in the UK, are supported far more by locals than by outsiders.

There are 15 inhabited islands as well as the Mainland, and a lot of wild beautiful emptiness; forget Google Maps and get a proper map. There are Nature and RSPB Reserves like the Noup Cliffs, prehistoric sites like Mousa Broch (by boat) and Jarlshof near Sumburgh, but St Ninian's Isle and Muckle Flugga are outposts among many you go to explore yourself. Shetland's potentially bright green future in renewables and initiatives like the Space Station on Unst put a whole new perspective on the value of its empty lands and limitless sea. Moving from wide-open space to energy hubs and Outer Space might be a challenge, but there is a lot of room.

SHETLAND ISLANDS

20 miles

20 kilometres

ATLANTIC OCEAN

NORTH ROE
③
▲ Ronas Hill

④
ST MAGNUS
BAY

TOFT

ULSTA

YELL SOUND

YELL

GUTCHER **BELMONT**

HAROLDSWICK

UNST

⑥

FETLAR

OUT SKERRIES

NORTH SEA

WHALSAY

BRAE
Busta House 🚤 🍴 Frankie's

MUCKLE ROE

PAPA STOUR

MAINLAND

WALLS
Burrastow House 🛏️

FOULA

Tingwall Airport
✈️

Maryfield House Hotel

SCALLOWAY

① **LERWICK**
(see inset)

BRESSAY

Mousa Broch 🏰 **MOUSA**

②

Jarlshof Prehistoric & Norse Settlement

SUMBURGH
⚓

Sumburgh Roost

↓ KIRKWALL, ORKNEY   ↓ ABERDEEN

Inset:

🍴 Mareel Café

Bressay →

⑤
The Dowry 🍴

Peerie Shop Café

🛏️ The Lerwick Hotel

LERWICK

Photo locations
1 Lerwick
2 St Ninian's Isle
3 Lang Ayre Beach
4 Dore Holm
5 Up Helly Aa
6 Muckle Flugga

LERWICK

60°9'12"N, 1°8'33"W

By plane you arrive on Shetland at Sumburgh, 27 miles to the south. By the overnight ferry from Aberdeen (or via Orkney), you wake up (hopefully not from a bumpy journey across the Pentland Firth), at the Holmsgarth Terminal, two miles from town. Lerwick's waterfront lies beneath the imposing Town Hall, which flies the Shetland flag, a squared-up version of the Saltire (though the same shade of blue). Bressay, behind us from this viewpoint, shelters Lerwick from the storms and is probably the reason Lerwick became Shetland's fishing and smuggling (gin, brandy, tobacco) central. A short frequent ferry and you're on your first other island.

Scalloway, a few miles away on the west coast, used to be Shetland's capital. The inhabitants there once burned the wooden waterfront to the ground. Later the passing French fleet had another go, but then Lerwick was rebuilt of sterner stuff: red granite and resolve. Now it is a proud and solidly Shetland town, both the most northerly and the most easterly in the British Isles.

Not unexpectedly Lerwick is both the cultural and commercial hub. Up Helly Aa and the highly regarded Folk Festival are here. The Peerie Café is one of the coolest café-culture places you could hang out in anywhere. There's much to explore in the alleyways, among the old stone houses familiar to fans of the *Shetland* TV series – the Lodberrie House in particular. Though it may be very far from the rest of the UK, this waterfront has a smell, a tune, an embrace of its own and a powerful sense of itself.

PHOTOGRAPH **PAUL TOMKINS**

ST NINIAN'S ISLE

59°58'18"N, 1°20'51"W

St Ninian's Isle is a curious offshore island north of Sumburgh and the seaway known as the Sumburgh Roost at the very south of Shetland. On the west coast, it faces the ocean.

The tiny island is only accessible at low tide. After camping overnight, Malcolm MacGregor's photograph was taken very early on a summer morning. St Ninian's is notable because the crescent beaches you cross to get there comprise the largest tombolo, or sandy isthmus, in Britain. Through the deposition of sand, the island becomes attached to the mainland and becomes a 'tied island'.

Shetland is full of topographically fascinating features like this. Mostly they go unnoticed and unreported, which makes them even more intriguing and open to discovery.

PHOTOGRAPH **MALCOLM MACGREGOR**

LANG AYRE BEACH

60°33'14"N, 1°28'14"W

Folk say this is 'the most amazing place on Shetland'. Its isolation, the fact that it can take three/four hours to get there (then back) will contribute to that perception. It is something of a pilgrimage, perhaps a bucket-list thing. The beach itself, stony with some sandy sections, is red from the granite cliffs and the hill above it. Two enigmatic jaggy islets, sit just offshore.

One of the reasons why it can take a while to get here is because, though you can walk round it, the given path leads first to a hill, Ronas, at 450 m the highest point on Shetland. Few hills anywhere can offer such a fine panorama of a whole region; in this case, it's like a seeing a whole country and its host of islands. On a good day you can see Saxa Vord Hill on Unst, the farthest high point north on Shetland; Fitful Head, almost the farthest sea point south, and even Fair Isle, 50 miles away.

An epic day out starts at Collafirth Hill on the A970, 30 miles north of Lerwick. To the summit of Ronas Hill it's about four miles but the terrain has its challenges – there's a rope to help your final descent down a small ravine to the beach. Lang Ayre is not even in many atlases and Google haven't been there either. But go and find it.

PHOTOGRAPH **NICK MCCAFFREY**

DORE HOLM

60°28'08"N, 1°36'11"W

Dore Holm is a magical rocky islet in the northwest of Shetland Mainland. A massive natural basalt arch, it has been likened to a giant waterhorse dipping deep into the sea. The Shetland pony just walked into the picture.

The holm is visible between Tangwick and Stenness at the end of the B9078, which comes off the left fork west on the A970 from Lerwick: about 30 miles. It's a long way for a look, but it could be combined with Lang Ayre Beach and Ronas Hill, on a very worthwhile day's outing, visiting three of the remarkable natural treasures to be found with just a little human effort in this glorious part of the world.

Philippe Clément is a Belgian internationally exhibited photographer.

PHOTOGRAPH **PHILIPPE CLÉMENT**

UP HELLY AA

60°9'18"N, 1°8'56"W

Unique to Shetland, Up Helly Aa is a spectacular party, where up to a thousand 'guizers' process through the streets of Lerwick with giant burning torches and then throw them into a replica of a Viking galley bonfire. They've been doing this since 1881 and, even with the advent of more recent health and safety regulations, which have put paid to many other traditional celebrations, Up Helly Aa goes from strength to strength.

For the 'Procession', the main event of a day which starts before dawn with the 'Proclamation' and goes on at ticketed parties and throughout the town well into the night, all the street lights are extinguished. For Shetlanders, whose winter nights are as long as their summer days, Up Helly Aa is a defining moment: their Norse past and the confident assertion of a living culture are different from and independent of anything on a distant Scottish mainland.

PHOTOGRAPH **ANDY BUCHANAN**

MUCKLE FLUGGA

60°51'20"N, 0°53'07"W

Muckle Flugga does sound like a muckle (big) far-flung place. Its name is from old Norse, meaning 'big steep-sided island'. Muckle Flugga is the most northerly lighthouse, the furthest human place in these many British Isles. For long-distance walk baggers, it makes John o'Groats seem like a halfway house.

The lighthouse was built by the Stevensons, of course Thomas and David, in 1854. It has 103 steps to the light. 200-ft waves crash over the summit of the rock from the unending sea. We might well ask: 'How on earth did they build that?'

I for one have never been to Muckle Flugga, but I appreciate its symbolic eminence in lighthouse lore and the entrenched ambition of Britannia to Rule the Waves. To get here, you must travel across Unst, where a Space Base will soon send rockets into the unending heavens. How on earth will we do that too?

Philippe Clément. After a long time he got his picture.

PHOTOGRAPH **PHILIPPE CLÉMENT**

SHETLAND: THE BEST OF

WHERE TO STAY

BURRASTOW HOUSE, WALLS www.burrastowhouse.co.uk 01595 809307. 40 mins from Lerwick out west. Peaceful Georgian house on quiet bay with views to the island of Vaila. Excellent cooking of fixed menu. • **BUSTA HOUSE, BRAE** www.bustahouse.com. 01806 522506. Historic country house hotel, 30 mins from Lerwick. Elegant and tranquil, lived-in. Good food and malts. Garden and beach walk. • **THE LERWICK HOTEL** www.shetlandhotels. 01595 692166. Possibly the best hotel in Lerwick for short stays and restaurant. Short walk to downtown. • **MARYFIELD HOUSE HOTEL, BRESSAY** www.maryfieldhousehotel.co.uk. 01595 820203. Great location though a 5-minute (v frequent) ferry hop from Lerwick (overlooks harbour). Destination restaurant.

WHERE TO EAT

THE DOWRY, LERWICK www.thedowry.co.uk. 01595 692373. 98 Commercial St. Contemporary restaurant bar and menu. Artisan coffee/beers etc • **PEERIE SHOP CAFÉ** www.peerieshop.co.uk. 01595 692816. Great very Shetland shop and café to snack and hang out. Home-made and baking. Near harbour. Daytime only. • **FRANKIE'S, BRAE.** www.frankiesfishandchips.com. 01806 522700. Takeaway and café. Award-winning fish 'n' chips, local seafood, home baking. Till 8 pm. • **MAREEL CAFÉ** www.mareel.org. 01595 745500. HD the café, restaurant of the Shetland Museum, Mareel adjacent part of Cinema arts centre. Both cultural and food hubs by harbour/waterfront, faced Covid challenges. Check current status first.

WHERE TO WALK

The author has not been able go walking on Shetland Mainland or the islands in recent years, so cannot personally propose options here. Recommended websites are: www.shetland.org, www.walkhighlands.co.uk.

THE SMALL ISLES

COLL

56°37′26″N, 6°31′35″W

Coll and Tiree go together, because they're on the same ferry route from Oban, but as islands they're very different. Coll has gentle hills, some trees, small sandy bays; it feels like a self-contained, self-assured place to live; everyone seems to know each other. Coll has declared itself 'unspoilt' and seems determined to remain so.

From the bay with its boats, Ross Evans, (one could say, the island's photographer) has taken a picture that looks across the village Arinagour to the parish church and the hotel, in many ways Coll's key buildings. As island hotels go, the Coll Hotel is in a league of its own, a fixture for all of 150 years, under the careful and conscientious ownership of the Oliphant family for the last 40. For visitors and locals alike, this hostelry is a haven. From its conservatory restaurant you look across the bay and the village and from its carefully tended garden, to Mull. Until 2021 I had never been to Coll. On a summer-long sojourn, Coll was the most pleasing discovery.

PHOTOGRAPH **ROSS EVANS**

COLL, MAIN STREET

56°37'29"N, 6°31'44"W

Arinagour is not a bustling wee village, but it beguiles us with an almost sleepy charm. Fewer than 50 folk live here on or around the main street. Red roofs add colour to the white. Most of what folk need can be found here in the shop and a cute post office, a good café/restaurant, fuel pumps, a cool bunk house and community centre and a pub at the hotel. There's no police or hospital, perhaps nobody ever breaks the law or a leg (though there is an airstrip for emergencies and posh arrivals).

Out of the village are roads to the ferry, south to the beaches, including the hidden delights around Crossapol Bay and the RSPB centre at Totronald, where the corncrake occasionally calls. Coll: the quiet tune of life and a comfy, civilized hotel. Let yourself go, there.

PHOTOGRAPH **ROSS EVANS**

TIREE

56°30'10"N, 6°53'37"W

Sand, sun and surf: to some they sum up Tiree. There's a lot more to it, of course, but the beaches of Tiree and the turquoise water can sometimes seem in another latitude. It is generally sunnier than the mainland and any of the other islands and in the last few years the surf's definitely up. The population's up too, as more people see the benefits of both the laid-back life and the entrepreneurial opportunities of a new kind of tourism powered by wind and water, and the culture that Tiree has nurtured. Tiree's programme of festivals is impressively true to the island's history and geography: the *Fèis*, the now long-established Music Festival, the Regatta, an agricultural show, the Tiree Wave Classic. It's all made in Tiree and it's authentic.

Tiree also has surprising stories to tell. The Skerryvore Lighthouse Museum at Hynish, the harbour and hotels around Scarinish and Gott Bay and even the airport in the centre of the island has a remarkable history. An airfield since 1929, it was a centre in the North Atlantic war effort with 2000 personnel stationed here. Now it brings Tiree closer, with direct flights to Glasgow.

But, as well as older culture gatherers and younger followers of the wind and wave, Tiree is a bright haven for families. The kid in Mike Rennie's photograph is his daughter. Like many other families, they come back to Tiree often to walk across that Machair to that sea.

PHOTOGRAPH **MIKE RENNIE**

TIREE, SURF'S UP

56°31'15"N, 6°57'26"W

The guy surfing this wave off Balevullin Beach is Ben Larg, living on Tiree and going places. He was a UK under-18 surf champion at the age of twelve. While he's the only figure in Mike's picture, there's a growing crew of others walking into the water. It includes men and women surfing their middle age. Some prefer to stay at the newly built surfer-friendly Reef Hotel by the airport rather than camp on a windy coast with the surfer tribe.

Balevullin has become a national destination for all Boarders: sail, surf and windsurf. The Tiree Wave Classic is the longest-established international windsurfing competition. Tiree is calling itself 'The Hawaii of the North', fanciful perhaps, but why not push the board out?

PHOTOGRAPH **MIKE RENNIE**

COLONSAY, KILORAN BEACH

56°06'14"N, 6°11'01"W

Colonsay, a haven of all small things Hebridean, has many charms and many beaches but Kiloran is its gem, the one that folk talk about with a wistful glint in the eye; it's often described as the finest in the islands. Low, craggy cliffs on one side and negotiable rocks and tiers of grassy dunes on the other. Colonsay – the whole island – was once bought as a picnic spot. Kiloran was probably the reason why!

But there is more to this perfectly proportioned island, only 10 miles by 2. Colonsay House has surprising botanical gardens brimming with rhododendrons, there's a very civilized hotel and pub, and a golf course that's over 200 years old. With birds atwitter in an often blue sky, the machair spread with flowers in spring and splendid sunsets because you're way out west, it's not surprising that people come back here all their lives.

PHOTOGRAPH **MATTHEW HART**

COLONSAY

56°01'46"N, 6°13'11"W

Colonsay, between Islay and Mull, small (10 by 4 miles) and enchanting, has been a well-kept secret, except perhaps for escapers from Edinburgh (and elsewhere) who've been coming here for years. Perhaps that's why there is a literary, a food/drink and a music festival. The ferry service – from Oban, 2 hrs 20, one a day but not every day, and Islay from Kennacraig – isn't particularly convenient but on a Wednesday it is possible, with planning, to come for a day trip. There's also a flight with Hebridean Air twice a week from Connel/Oban.

In some respects, Colonsay is for those of a more refined taste in island life, less rigorous, less vigorous. You can walk gently and cycle everywhere. The historic hotel and locals', bar is tasteful, the banter civilized, and the menu comes with a decent wine list. At Scalasaig, near the quay is a shop, a surprising bookshop and a café, the Pantry, where; the cottage community catch up on the gossip. The House Gardens are open to the public and then there's famed Kiloran Beach.

Michael's photograph here looks south across to tiny Oronsay, a tidal island. A picture of its extraordinary Priory is overleaf.

PHOTOGRAPH **MICHAEL STIRLING-AIRD**

ORONSAY, THE PRIORY

56°01'10"N, 6°15'18"W

About three miles south of Scalasaig, on an ambling walk or cycle, you reach the Strand, a tidal causeway which you can cross (after checking the tides) to visit Oronsay. Its, best to leave the bike and walk the 20 minutes to the ruins of the Augustinian Priory.

Not a huge amount is known of its origins. Perhaps on the site of an earlier church, it is thought that it was built c.1380 by John of Islay, the Lord of the Isles. In the 16th century, a distinct school of monumental sculpture flourished on Oronsay, as evidenced by two large Celtic crosses within the perimeter and slabs and effigies inside. There's a small topiary maze in the adjacent garden, so it's an interesting place to visit and, exploring further, you might encounter choughs and corncrakes, barnacle geese in winter and almost certainly grey seals. Over to Oronsay is a satisfying excursion.

PHOTOGRAPH **MICHAEL STIRLING-AIRD**

BUTE

55°52'47"N, 5°04'42"W

Driving north out of Tighnabruaich on the A8003 in the heart of Argyll, we come to one of Scotland's great views. Spread out before us is the breathtaking watery vista of the Kyles of Bute. Round the head of the short sea loch there, we come upon the Kyles and the crossing at Colintraive on the few-minutes, ferry to ease gently into the understated ambience of the Isle of Bute. The more usual route to and from Glasgow and the rest of the world is the always friendly ferry crossing from Wemyss Bay. That way you're bang into Rothesay.

For some, Bute is Rothesay: a seaside/Clydeside town, the Pavilion and the Victorian Toilets, the West End's fish 'n' chips and, south out of town, amazing Mount Stuart and its grounds. These are, if you like, the tourist attractions. But Bute can also boast of its beaches: Kilchattan Bay beyond Mount Stuart, Kerrycroy, Scalpsie Bay and, north of that, ethereal Ettrick Bay, and its famous tearoom.

What's important to remember about Bute, not so far from Glasgow, is that it's a rural, almost bucolic place. There are forgiving hills (Windy Hill the highest at 913 ft) and farms and village pubs. These cows could be anywhere, but they are the contented cows of Bute. Cowal is behind them.

PHOTOGRAPH **DOUGLAS CORRANCE**

BUTE, MOUNT STUART

55°47'39"N, 5°01'51"W

One of Scotland's secret jewels, this astounding Victorian Gothic house on the Isle of Bute, with magnificent gardens and woodlands that stretch to the Clyde, makes for a perfect day out. The House echoes the passion for mythology, astronomy, astrology and religion of the third Marquis in fascinating detail. Contemporary art commissions in the grounds and the strikingly modern visitor centre complement the Bute collection of masterpieces. And the Gardens: Kitchen, Rock, 'The Wee' and the Pinetum are all a joy too. Leave your humdrum life behind, everything here is in the best possible taste.

PHOTOGRAPH **PHILIP LOVEL**

EASDALE ISLAND

56°17'35"N, 5°39'17"W

Easdale is a minute's ferry hop from the Island of Seil, which is more a peninsula that hangs into the Firth of Lorn from the Argyll coast south of Oban. Extraordinary Easdale is one of the 'Slate Islands', the source and centre of Scotland's slate industry, which once roofed the world from Melbourne to Nova Scotia. Mines used to extend 300 feet below sea level until the Great Storm of 1850 flooded most of the quarries. Today, as can be clearly seen from Iain Masterton's aerial photograph, the pools remain a unique topographical feature. They're great for summer swimming.

Tiny Easdale can be the centre of a big day out, truly like nowhere else, and it's all around you. On Luing, a larger island, a three-minute ferry journey away, the Atlantic Islands Centre tells the fascinating story of the rise and fall of slate evocatively well. On Easdale there's a folk museum and a tearoom/pub on a couthie village green.

By this perspective we can see what a difference a drone makes.

PHOTOGRAPH **IAIN MASTERTON**

CUMBRAE

55°46'08"N, 4°54'58"W

There is more than one Cumbrae. This is the Greater, the one that generations of west-coast tourists have come to for the beach, maybe a dook and the ice-cream – a peach melba at the legendary Ritz Café (under different owners, but still there). Ten minutes by ferry from Largs, Millport on Cumbrae was the port of call going 'Doon the Water' in the Glasgow Fair Fortnight. Cumbrae's salty air also comes with a heady tang of nostalgia.

Millport's sandy bay takes up most of the south coast, but the other great delight of Cumbrae is that you can get round the island in an easy walk and, especially, on a bike. The highest point in the middle of the island, marked by the Glaid Stone (a naturally occurring stone) is a doddle. This photograph is from the Glaid Stone road, looking back to the bay. Through the trees you can see the Cathedral of the Isles, the smallest cathedral in Europe, one of the architect Butterfield's great works – another is Keble College, Oxford. The College of the Holy Spirit here has been an Episcopalian retreat since 1884. In spring the surrounding grounds are a profusion of white wild garlic. The joy of the human spirit has always been here too on blessed little Great Cumbrae.

PHOTOGRAPH **KENNY WILLIAMSON**

GIGHA

55°40'58"N, 5°45'15"W

Between Islay and the Mull of Kintyre, and with a ferry port down the peninsula at Tayinloan, Gigha is not the easiest of islands to get to. But the journey is only 20 minutes and everything you might expect of an island except hills is here on your west-coast doorstep: a friendly island hotel with a bar and restaurant, an excellent bistro/café at the pier at Ardminish Bay, botanical gardens at Achamore House and great beaches, including a double beach where the Queen once swam off the Royal Yacht *Britannia* (it says here in a previous edition of *Scotland the Best*).

In Gigha there's no traffic, no crowds. Paul Tomkins's photograph was taken at the north point of the island. In the dawn light he has captured an atmosphere you can only feel on an island. Gigha sits in its own kind of precious isolation, farther south than all the other small Scottish islands.

PHOTOGRAPH **PAUL TOMKINS**

HANDA ISLAND

58°22'49"N, 5°11'19"W

If you have even a passing interest in or affection for birds, there's nowhere better to be than here on a long summer's day. In Sutherland, a long way from the city, Handa is nevertheless just off the A894 (and the dreaded by some, North Coast 500). It's north of Scourie and then by small boat from Tarbet (summer only).

Handa is an island of national importance, a nature reserve managed by the Scottish Wildlife Trust. To the south is Boulder Bay and a beach for seal searching and whale watching. But the wonders of Handa are revealed on a 1.5-mile walk over herb-rich grassland protected occasionally by slatted wooden trackways, to the 100-m-high cliffs of red Torridonian Sandstone, covered in seabirds. Behold the puffins, kittiwakes, fulmers and the biggest colonies of razorbills and guillemots in the UK. Giant skuas patrol the skies, eider ducks and oystercatchers dot the sea. But you don't have to be a birdwatcher to be in awe of nature on this green gem of an island.

PHOTOGRAPH **VINCENT LOWE**

EIGG

56°53'38"N, 6°09'37"W

Rum, Eigg and Muck, in order of size, make up 'The Small Isles', as they're known, especially if you're on a boat on the usual routes from Mallaig or Arisaig. Eigg is the most accessible for a fulfilling day or short visit: convenient ferry times allow time to explore, a choice of inexpensive places to stay, a café and shop at the pier and a welcoming feeling from a very well-organized local community. They'll show you how to get to the Bay of Laig, the many other walks and nooks and crannies and this, the splendid Sgùrr an Eigg. Eigg was taken in house as it were, by the Eigg Trust in 1997. Since 2008, it's been disconnected from the mainland and self-sustainable in renewable energy. Every aspect of the island runs to a uniquely green agenda.

From the ferry pier, the route with a straightforward path on to the ridge is about 5 miles (3/4 hours, there is a bit of scrambling along the top). The views of all the small isles, Skye and the mainland are magnificent. On a good day, exceeding all expectations, there's no better perch in the Inner Hebrides.

PHOTOGRAPH **ALLAN WRIGHT**

EIGG, LAIG BAY, AND RUM

56°55'01"N, 6°09'36"W

Laig Bay is one of the great beaches of the Hebrides. Wide and white silver overlaid on black sand, its character different every day. However it's not all sand. Part of the littoral, as in Julian Calverley's image, is a stratified rock foreshore with pools that capture the light. Photographers love this bay because the shoreline and the infinite interplay of sand and sea lends itself to artistic perspectives, even abstraction.

But the beach is alluring for other reasons. It can seem vast, often there's nobody else here and it's pristine. There is the classic view of Rum. Though three miles away, its mountains, looming large and mysterious, seem close. From Eigg pier it's a 2.5-mile walk to Cleadale and the beach (there's also a minibus, there and/or back). The 'Singing Sands', a much smaller, squeaky beach is to the north while Laig is to the south, left from the end of the road.

PHOTOGRAPH **JULIAN CALVERLEY**

MUCK

56°50'09"N, 6°14'45"W

Muck is quite the smallest of the Small Isles (Eigg, Rum and Canna), seen here in a rosy glow at sunset. It's an island you feel you have the run of, as if it was yours, even though it is actually owned by the MacEwen family. They are the most beneficent of lairds, Lawrence is affectionately known as the Prince of Muck, and a film about him and his efforts to preserve the island's fragile ecosystem was made in 2021. His daughter and son-in-law run Gallanach Lodge – excellent bespoke accommodation and dining near the beach – the red building in the photograph.

The main activity of Muck, apart from looking after its visitors, is sheep rearing and making things from the wool. There are just over 20 inhabitants. You arrive at the pier (Port Mòr), where there's a tearoom and the (only) road to Gallanach less than two miles away. The highest hill is Beinn Airein at 449 ft. There are good walks but, oddly, you can get almost scarily lost (at least I once did). Porpoises and seals pop up in the ever-surrounding ocean. That's all you need to know really. Now go get lost in Muck.

PHOTOGRAPH **DALZIEL**

THE SHIANTS

57°53'31"N, 6°21'17"W

In The Minch, east of Harris, five miles southeast of Lewis, the Shiants are two small islands in a big ocean (and a group of rocks to the west), the only islands in this book that are not readily accessible by public transport. But it is possible to hire boats to go there and there is a well-maintained bothy, where you're welcome to stay for free.

Once owned by writer Compton Mackenzie of *Whisky Galore* fame, since 1937 the archipelago has been in the hands and care of the Nicolson family – first Nigel, then Adam, both writers, now grandson Tom. Adam Nicolson wrote the island classic, *Sea Room*, about it. More recently, Robert Macfarlane also wrote of them in his best-selling book, *The Old Ways*. There seems to be something otherworldly about the Shiants, apparent from your arrival at this anchorage on the main island Eilean an Taighe, the Enchanted Isle. A huge congregation of puffins summer on the hillside of Garbh Eilean, which rises above the bay. Macfarlane writes how they were greeted with 'an amplified riffle, like banknotes whirred through a telling machine – the compounded wing-noise of thousands of puffins crisscrossing the sky'.

But alighting here is not just for writers, photographers and ornithologists. The Shiants are for all pure island lovers – read the books and dream of them.

PHOTOGRAPH **JIM RICHARDSON**

Peter Irvine was born in Jedburgh in the Borders and educated at Hawick High School and Edinburgh University. He has been the creator and director of many of Scotland's major events and festivals including The Opening of the Scottish Parliament in 1999 and Edinburgh's Hogmanay from it's inception in 1993 to 2017. He lives in Edinburgh's New Town. Peter was awarded an MBE for services to Scotland and an Honorary Doctorate from the Open University.

PHOTOGRAPH **PHOEBE GRIGOR**

PHOTO CREDITS

cover, pages 8–9, 65, 93, 119, 165, 179, 181, 183, 239
  © Jim Richardson
inside front cover, 23, 71, 237, inside back cover © Dalziel
pages 14–15, 27, 42–43, 47, 83, 155 © Richard Cross,
  www.richardx.co.uk
pages 17, 19, 45 © Mhairi Law
pages 21, 37, 49, 61, 69, 79, 81, 113, 117, 169, 193, 229
  © Paul Tomkins
pages 25, 217, 219 © Michael Stirling-Aird
pages 33, 35, 51, 53, 63, 73 © John Maher
pages 39, 41, 94–95, 235 © Julian Calverley, www.juliancalverley.com
page 59 © Stefan Auth / Alamy
pages 67, 195 © Malcolm MacGregor
pages 85, 109, 159, 177, 221 © Douglas Corrance
page 87 © Lucilla Noble / Courtesy of Eilean Iarmain
page 89 © David Eustace – All Rights Reserved
page 91 © Marcus McAdan / Scottish Viewpoint
pages 97, 99, 101 © Cailean MacLean
page 107 © Angus McComiskey
page 111 © Sven Stroop
page 115 © David Lomax / Robert Harding Picture Library Ltd
page 121 © Les Gibbon

pages 127, 133 © Mark Unsworth / Islay Studios
pages 128, 137 © Ben Shakespeare Photography
pages 130–131 © George Robertson
pages 135, 139 © Jack Harding
page 141 © Colin Palmer
page 143 © Euan Myles
pages 149, 151, 157 © Andy Surridge
page 153 © Joe Dunckley
page 167 © Alistair Peebles / Pier Art Centre
pages 171, 173, 175 © Rebecca Marr
pages 185, 187 © Ingrid Budge
page 197 © Nick McCafferty
pages 199, 202–203 © Clement Philippe
page 201 © Andy Buchanan / Alamy
pages 207, 209 © Ross Evans
pages 211, 213 © Mike Rennie
page 215 © Matthew Hart / Alamy
page 223 © Philip Lovel / Courtesy of Mount Stuart
page 225 © Ian Masterton
page 227 © Kenny Williamson
page 231 © Vincent Lowe
page 233 © Allan Wright